THE DEVIL
AT HOME

THE DEVIL AT HOME

I ALWAYS KNEW MY HUSBAND HAD A DARK SIDE. BUT THEN HE TRIED TO KILL ME.

RACHEL WILLIAMS

with ELLIE PIOVESANA

EBURY
PRESS

1 3 5 7 9 10 8 6 4 2

Ebury Press, an imprint of Ebury Publishing
20 Vauxhall Bridge Road
London SW1V 2SA

Ebury Press is part of the Penguin Random House group of companies whose
addresses can be found at global.penguinrandomhouse.com

 Penguin
Random House
UK

First published by Ebury Press in 2018

www.penguin.co.uk

A CIP catalogue record for this book is available from the British Library

ISBN 9781785037658

Typeset in 11.25/16 pt Adobe Garamond Pro
by Integra Software Services Pvt. Ltd, Pondicherry

Printed and bound in Great Britain by Clays Ltd, St Ives PLC

 Penguin Random House is committed to a sustainable future
for our business, our readers and our planet. This book is
made from Forest Stewardship Council® certified paper.

For my sons

Foreword

By actor, Michael Sheen

The story you are holding in your hands is shocking. It shouldn't exist. It should never be allowed to happen to anyone. And we all share responsibility.

At the same time, Rachel's story is transformative. It is life-changing. Not just for Rachel herself but, potentially, for the thousands upon thousands of people whose lives are affected by domestic violence and abuse every day in this country. Those who suffer it directly or indirectly, and those who perpetrate it. And, perhaps most importantly, for our whole society.

Because this is a story of a society that is getting it wrong. Rachel describes it as an epidemic and the figures suggest she is right. Domestic violence is not something we find easy to talk about and understandably so. It reveals aspects of our society and ourselves that we'd prefer not to face or acknowledge. But not having the courage to look at who we really are and what is really going on in too many of our families and relationships only serves those who are violent and controlling. It leaves those who are on the receiving end of it isolated and unprotected.

As Rachel's story shows, people who are suffering such horrendous experiences display almost unimaginable levels of strength and courage to survive and come through to the other side. We must all do whatever we can as a society to support people like Rachel on that journey. Too often, though, our institutions and systems are letting us down in doing that, compounding the problems rather than serving the needs of the vulnerable. Not necessarily by design but often through lack of awareness or outdated systemic responses, people who need real help are given obstacles instead of support. All the more reason to make sure that this story is heard, that the true scale of the issue is reckoned with and our task of re-imagining an effective response is faced up to and implemented.

Rachel is incredibly brave in sharing her story with such honesty and directness. Not only here in this book but also constantly putting herself out there in the media, on social media and in her various ambassador roles to keep pushing for change. Telling her story will undoubtedly save lives and I hope will provide a major step towards the societal transformation we so desperately require.

As I said at the beginning, this story is a shocking one. It lays bare one of the darkest moments of Rachel's life and I honestly don't know how I or anyone I know would ever cope with such horrific events. But Rachel and her story are so much more than that. I've had the great pleasure to meet and talk with Rachel on many occasions and it is her generosity, her determination and her optimism that shine through more than anything. This is a story full of hope and strength. Rachel has found a way to turn the horror and the loss of her darkest times into a call for change. She is fighting every day to make things better, to give support where it is needed and to draw attention to where we are letting people down who most need our help.

No one is better suited to this mighty task than the extraordinary woman whose story you have in your hands but we must all look to what we can each do to aid her in this struggle.

We must show a small drop of that courage that Rachel and others like her have shown, dare to face ourselves and what we allow, and then work together to create the change.

Michael Sheen

Prologue

For the first time in six weeks, I woke up in my own bed. It was Friday, and I could sense the warm air on the other side of the curtains before I was even fully awake. I stretched and opened my eyes. The house was quiet. It would be ages until the boys surfaced.

My bedroom drawers were still in a pile next to my bed so I climbed out and quietly slotted each of them back into place. Then I went downstairs to make myself a coffee. As the kettle boiled I wondered whether or not to eat breakfast. But the knot in my stomach wasn't hunger, it was fear.

I took my coffee upstairs, switched on the TV in my room, and climbed back into bed like I always did to sit and do my make-up with the news on in the background. I picked up my hand mirror and paused to look at the woman staring back. My hair was a short bob now – the longest it had been in years – and my face looked slimmer too. I felt good. I felt strong. I felt like a bird who was about to fly. The cage door was finally open but it wasn't quite time to go through it. There was something holding me back.

Hair and make-up done, I threw on some jeans with a new top and the shiny black loafers I'd bought as a treat from Clarks a few weeks earlier. I drank the last of my coffee, brushed my teeth and went back to the kitchen to make a quick sandwich before leaving the house around 8.40am. I liked to get to the salon early so I could get the kettle on before the morning rush. I didn't normally work Fridays but had been asked to cover as a favour. The salon was only a short walk from my house, but knowing how strained things were with my husband Darren, I took my car and parked outside. After living with him for 18 years, giving myself the means to escape had become second nature.

When I arrived at the salon my boss Carol was already inside.

'Morning,' she chirped as I walked in.

'Beautiful, isn't it?' I smiled.

'How are you feeling?'

'Fine,' I replied automatically.

I wasn't fine and we both knew it, but I wanted to be at work, to be around people. Keeping busy had always been my coping mechanism.

It was a typical Friday morning at the salon – back-to-back appointments and regulars coming and going, getting their hair done ready for the weekend. The sun continued to beam through the shop windows, and before I knew it, it was 1.30pm.

Between clients I nipped out the back to call my sister Natalie. I'd heard that Darren might have had an appointment with a psychiatrist and wondered if she'd noticed his Land Rover parked outside the clinic when she passed that morning. She didn't answer, but rang back around 2pm to say she hadn't seen it. My heart sank. I'd really hoped he was getting help because without it the slim chance of him ever leaving me alone seemed even less likely.

Back on the shop floor, Mrs Rogers was under the dryer and Carol was seeing to my next customer Connie, a wonderful old dear in her nineties. I cut her hair and blow-dried it just how she liked it. When we were done I took her to the till so she could pay. We were chatting away as I handed over her change when all of a sudden the salon went dark. I glanced at the front windows. Something was blocking the sunlight – something big. It was Darren. The six foot seven, 23-stone frame I knew so well filled every inch of the doorway. My blood ran cold as he pushed open the door and stepped inside. He had a sports bag in his hand and he was reaching inside it. He was pulling out a long, silver shotgun.

Before I had time to think, my feet were carrying me towards him. I had my arms outstretched, ready to grab the weapon, to stop whatever he was planning to do.

'For fuck's sake, Da!' I screamed. 'Think of Jack!'

There was a struggle, then a crack to my forehead as he struck me with the butt of the gun. The blow knocked me to the ground and I came to with Connie lying right next to me. She had either fallen or thrown herself on the floor next to me and was now screaming at Darren to get away from me: 'Go on with you! Get out!'

In the commotion, the reception desk had toppled over onto its side. I grabbed it and pulled it towards me as some sort of cover, only for the heel of Darren's boot to kick it straight out of my grasp. He was right above me now. He had the gun in his hands and he was aiming at my chest.

Darren shouted: 'I love you, Rachel!'

This is it, I thought. I closed my eyes, pulled my knees up to my chest and he fired.

Rachel I know I can be
a bit weird and crazy insecure
etc etc, but I would walk to
the end of the earth for you
give all my blood for you
and draw my last breath to save
my lovelly, lovelly Wife.
    You are the 1 the only 1,

I KNOW THAT I SHOULD SAY THIS
MUCH MORE OFTEN THAN I do...

love   you in this
life and the next.
    forever your's
    Darren X X X
           X X X.

Chapter One

It's bedtime, I'm two years old and my favourite person in the whole world is tucking me into a bottom bunk. It's my big strong grandad – or Grancha, as I called him – and he's singing to me lovingly, trying to soothe me to sleep. *Go to sleep, my baby, shut your big brown eyes ...*

This is my earliest memory, living on Cyril Street in Newport, Wales, with my mum's parents – Grancha and my hilarious nanna Dolly. I adored them both and they absolutely doted on me. I lived with my grandparents because my mum Avril, who slept above me on the top bunk, was just a kid herself when she had me.

To say I was a surprise would be a bit of an understatement. When she fell pregnant at 17, Mum was so terrified of disappointing her father she kept the whole pregnancy a secret. For the whole nine months, no one in the family had the slightest clue I was on the way until the day I was born. When I arrived kicking and screaming on 10 February 1972, it was a huge shock to the family and no doubt the talk of the town. But Mum stood her ground. She wanted me, so everyone pulled together to support her and give me the best possible start they could.

I was still a toddler when my mum and dad Ray got their own house on Bishton Street. It was number 33 and less than two minutes' walk from Nanna and Grancha's, which was perfect for everyone. The house needed a bit of work, but Grancha was only too happy to roll up his sleeves and help knock it into shape. His father had been a real handyman, making built-in wardrobes before the rest of the world even knew what they were. Now Grancha was the one who could turn his hand to any and every type of DIY. He had the most incredible shed and whenever he went out there I wouldn't be far behind him, eager for a mooch around his treasure trove. I was obsessed! I loved looking at the tools and messing about with all the noisy little tins full of different nuts and bolts. Other girls my age were into pretty pink dresses and dollies in pushchairs. I was the chubby tomboy hanging out down the shed wearing Grancha's flat cap.

We were an incredibly close-knit family and I was so lucky that Nanna and Grancha were always around to help out. When I started nursery, they would take it in turns to walk me over George Street Bridge and hug me goodbye at the gate. I never cried when I was dropped off – I was the one marching inside and getting on with things. In the area where we hung our coats up we had a locker each with our own toothbrush and flannel inside.

Mum and Dad got married, and in 1977, when I was five, they gave me a baby sister. The day they brought her home from the hospital I stood on my tippy toes and peered into the pram to get a look at little baby Natalie. She seemed to sleep a lot, but also made a lot of noise when she wanted to. I thought she was wonderful – a real live dolly!

Coming from a family of strong characters gave me a great deal of confidence as I started to make my way in the world. I left nursery and moved up to Maindee Primary School where I blossomed into a right little madam. Because I was so extroverted, the teachers loved me and I always had a gang of mates around me. My favourite time of day was playtime because we were always itching to get outside and play Kiss, Cuddle or Torture. This involved being chased around by boys and, if one managed to get hold of you, you had to tell him whether you wanted a kiss, a cuddle or to be tortured. I never found out what the torture option involved because I always asked for a cuddle or a kiss. Some of them would try to go for the lips and we would run away screaming. The boys were generally quite scared of us, but I managed to get one of them to be my boyfriend for a while. His name was Michael, he was in my class and lived at 101 Chepstow Road. We didn't talk much, but there was a lot of cute hand holding. Michael broke my heart by emigrating to Australia with his family.

As I moved up through the school I got a reputation as a bit of a chatterbox. I loved to talk so much that, if the receptionist ever called in sick, the head, Mr Madden, would pull me out of class to sit and answer the phones. I felt so smug strutting off out of my classroom to do a grown-up job.

The cane was still around in those days and there were always whispers in the playground that Mr Madden had some in his office. Being the nosy parker I was, I decided I was going to find out if it was true. I snuck over to his office and peered through the keyhole of the locked door. I gasped when I saw that, sure enough, there were rows of thin brown wooden canes lined up neatly on his wall. Feeling like the bee's knees, I ran back to the playground to tell everyone the rumours were true.

The way I'm describing myself, you would think I'd be one of those kids who loved the limelight. Yet when it came to things like the school nativity, I much preferred to be on the sidelines doing something practical like opening and closing the curtains. I wasn't a fan of the stage at all. There was something about the lights being in my eyes and not being able to see the faces of the audience properly that I found really daunting. Anyway, I had bigger fish to fry.

One day after our school dinner they brought out the most disappointing dessert I'd ever seen in my life – two measly slices of tinned peach and a bit of evaporated milk. I looked down at my bowl and thought: *Is that it?* That afternoon I went straight home and complained to my mother.

'Why don't you write a letter?' she suggested.

'I will!' I said, defiant.

So that night, I sat and wrote a letter to Mr Madden, explaining how I was still hungry after my lunch because two slices of peach was not even close to a substantial pudding. It just wasn't good enough! Next morning I hand-delivered the letter to Mr Madden's office and, after calling me in for a chat, he agreed to increase the portion sizes. I like to think of it as my *Oliver* moment – *please, sir, I want some more!* Even then I was on a mission for change.

I was from a working-class family living hand to mouth, yet my sister Nat and I didn't want for anything. Every birthday and Christmas we got a huge pile of presents, and each and every summer we went on a family holiday. One year we went to Cornwall and stayed in a little chalet. When I think back to that holiday, my memory of the weather is that the sun didn't stop shining the whole time we were there. Mum and Dad bought us a dinghy and we spent hours splashing about in it at the beach. We didn't need much to have fun.

Mum and Dad were still young and very sociable so many a Saturday afternoon was spent at Pillgwenlly Sports Club. The grown-ups enjoyed a drink with their mates while me and Nat mucked about, bowling and playing skittles. Sunday was all about Mum's roast dinner in the oven and a good family film on the telly, usually James Bond or Bruce Lee. I couldn't have asked for a better childhood. Life was good, but that's not to say it was all plain sailing.

Mum and Dad bickered from time to time and there were a couple of big rows that woke us up in the night, prompting Nat to crawl into bed next to me, feeling frightened.

'It's OK,' I would tell her. 'Just go back to sleep.'

When I was 11, I was walking home from the park when my nanna came running up the street.

'Now I don't want you to panic, Rachel,' she said, clearly panicking.

I peered past her and down the road to see an ambulance outside our house.

'Grancha's hit your father,' she said.

I ran home to see my dad being carried out on a stretcher, his head all bandaged up. Unbeknownst to me there had been a heated row and Dad had slapped my mother so hard it perforated her eardrum. When Grancha got wind of it, he marched round to ours to confront Dad. They had words out in the street which ended with Grancha grabbing a plank of wood out of a skip and beating Dad over the head with it. There were nails sticking out of the wood and he was left with a couple of big holes in his scalp.

To this day he still has the scars. To his credit, Dad took the beating and never pressed charges. He knew he was in the wrong and no doubt imagined himself reacting the same way if a man ever hurt me or Nat.

I didn't come from a violent family, but they were people who believed you stuck up for yourself and your own. They had each other's backs and were a tough, resilient bunch who never let the world get the better of them. I believe that their strength and positive attitude rubbed off on me and, years later, probably helped save my life.

The fight between Dad and my mother wasn't something that was ever discussed in front of me, but I was smart enough to know that what Dad had done was serious enough to deserve the beating from Grancha. In the weeks that followed, I learnt that hitting a woman was serious enough to end a marriage, too. They never told us they were divorcing, Dad simply moved out. We never saw Mum get upset, which I think, all credit to her, must have been why we never felt worried or unsettled.

Grancha helped Mum pay the mortgage for about a year after that, so we wouldn't have to move house. For a while, Dad would visit on a Sunday and take Nat and me out for the day, but then it just stopped and we didn't see him for years. I never held any resentment towards him, though. Things were great when he was around, then when he left we were still happy and secure in our little family unit: life just went on.

Shortly after Dad left, me, Mum and Nat went abroad for the very first time. It had been booked before the break-up so Mum invited a girlfriend in Dad's place. It was a lovely holiday to Spain and I was obviously really excited to go on a plane, but I was almost twelve now and due to start my first year at Lliswerry High School. The end of the holiday clashed with the start of school and I was gutted. I knew everyone would be catching up with friends and making new ones and at the time it felt gut-wrenching to be missing out.

I needn't have worried, though. Despite joining a few days late, it wasn't long before I was in the swing of high school, relishing the boost it gave my social life. There were new faces at the park after school and there was the excitement of buying and trying cigarettes. I remember me and one friend smoking a cheeky fag in a bush just in case anyone we knew walked past. We were puffing away when I heard someone shout, 'I'll tell your mother!' I panicked and shouted back, 'It's not me!'

Mum was the only one in our family who smoked and it was mostly a social thing. She had been known to send me to the shop to buy her a packet of ten, but I knew she'd batter me if she found out I'd been smoking myself. She'd have been one of those mothers who made you smoke 20 in a row so you couldn't even look at a fag again, so I was always very careful not to get caught.

As a teenager, I was still a tomboy who loved to be outdoors, but now I was doing it with a full face of make-up. I've loved make-up for as long as I can remember. Nanna Dolly always had the most amazing skin and I'm sure it was her who encouraged me to look after mine. She used to tell me to drink the water that the cabbage had been boiling in. It sounds gross but I quite liked it! Anything to keep me beautiful! Nanna Dolly also swore by Nivea face cream so, as soon as I started getting one or two pounds a week pocket money, that's what I would buy – Nivea face cream, cheap sachets of face mask or a copy of *Jackie* magazine. When we had no money left, me and my girlfriends would steal lipsticks from Boots. I mastered a nifty trick of dropping them into my umbrella.

I had to get an eight o'clock bus to school so, if I wanted to look my best, I had to start early. Every morning I would get up at six, have a shower and wash my hair. Mum would make me tea and toast and I'd take it back to bed where I would sit making myself look perfect for school. My face would get the full works then I would style my hair with giant flicks at the sides, Farrah Fawcett style. I still have an old bus pass somewhere and in the photo I have the most bouffant wings and perfectly lined lips you've ever seen.

I went through a brief phase of wanting to be a punk, which mostly consisted of massacring T-shirts with a hole punch. I kept my hair long on top and got Mum to shave the back right into my neck, like a long version of a flat top. I was always dyeing it with cheap wash-in wash-out colours. I even tried pink food colouring once, which was great until it rubbed off all over my pillow.

Mum never minded me experimenting as she was young herself and always one to take care of her appearance. She wore nice clothes and liked to put her face on and do her hair. If she couldn't afford the hairdresser's she would put a colour on herself at home. I remember one of the first boys I brought home seeing her and going, 'Phwoar! Your mum's fit!' It was a bit weird to hear, but I remember thinking, *Yeah, I suppose she is!* It was the first time I heard a boy comment about my mother in that way, but it certainly wasn't the last.

It's hardly surprising then that Mum wasn't single for long. She struck up a close friendship with Colin, a welder who lived a few doors down. Nat and me liked him a lot, and, although Mum never openly said that they were in a relationship, she did ask if we minded him moving in. Once she knew we were OK with it, he was officially part of the family.

I was – and still am – very similar to my mum. I like everything to be just so. For example, on a Sunday I'd spend hours painting my nails then I would get my school uniform all laid out neatly ready for the next day. Natalie was the complete opposite. She was the messy one and woe betide you if you used the bathroom after her. Once she started wearing make-up and using hairspray to tame her wild wavy hair, the bathroom mirror would be caked in it. We shared a room and it was so obvious which side of the room belonged to who it was almost comical.

Sunday was 'hoover and polish' day and we were expected to do our share, in our room at the very least.

I'd ask Nat, 'Are you hoovering or polishing?'

'I'm not doing anything!' she'd whine.

'Well,' I'd snap, 'it's one or the other. Take your pick.'

She would then ignore me until I was so wound up I would swing for her.

'You're doing something!' I would scream at her. 'You're such a scruffy mare!'

Despite the sisterly rows we were always close. She looked up to me and I liked the authority. If I was in the mood I'd let her tag along with me to meet my mates down the park. I don't remember it but she swears I made her start smoking.

'You put a fag in my mouth,' she says to this day.

I always reply, 'Well, you didn't have to suck it, did you!'

I had a big circle of friends and on Saturdays we would go to Kemp or Jubilee Park where a lot of the older kids would congregate. We would all chip in for cider and cigarettes and throw our own little party. You could buy single cigarettes back then so, if there wasn't enough in the kitty for ten fags, we'd get as many as we could afford and share them round.

My best friend in the world was Rachael Phillips. She was ballsy, pretty and loved her make-up like me. We looked so grown up that by the time we were 15 we had no problem getting served in the pubs. On Tuesdays and Wednesdays it was pound a pint night at The Carpenter's Arms. We would get the bus there and have two pints of bitter each while chatting to all the old boys. God, I loved to talk! Stinking of booze and fags, we'd get the last bus home. I'd open the front door, shout, 'I'm going up to bed!' and leg it straight upstairs so Mum wouldn't smell the pub on me.

Rachael and I spent so much time together we became known as The Two Rachels. Her parents lived in a posh house that had a bar downstairs. We would sneak in, fill up a milk bottle with a shot from each of the optics and take it down the park to get drunk. I don't know where the hell I got it from but I had this black cigarette holder. With my long nails, my red lipstick and my cigarette in a holder I swear I thought I was Joan Collins.

After one particularly boozy gathering, I stayed over at Rachael's and when we got into bed the room started spinning. We didn't want to wake her parents by going into the bathroom to be sick, so we did it out the window. The next morning, her mum came in, opened the curtains and saw the whole sorry mess all over the roof below.

I had fun, but was always careful not to push my luck too far, especially with Mum. We clashed occasionally, but I don't think I caused her too much bother. She had a tougher time with Natalie. One night, she lied that she was sleeping at a friend's house when in fact a group of them had planned to spend the night at the local cemetery. Well, you can imagine how creeped out they got in the dark. They ended up walking the streets and being picked up by the police. Mum was none too pleased to get a knock on the door from a copper in the middle of the night.

I somehow managed to keep a relatively low profile, despite being a bit of a ringleader at school. I always had my following, eager to join me round smoker's corner. We'd roll our knee-high socks down to our ankles and smother baby oil all over our legs to try to get a tan while we sat on the grass puffing away.

'I'm not going to maths today,' I'd announce nonchalantly.

'Oh, we'll come with you then,' they'd all say, and we would swan off down the park and wag the lesson. I don't know how we got away with it. I remember we hated the winter because we were always desperate to be outside but it just wasn't cool to wear a coat to school. I used to wear one of Dad's old knitted Aran jumpers instead. It was navy and looked dead smart with my pristine white shirt underneath.

When it came to boys, I didn't have a type looks-wise but my head would most definitely be turned by someone who could make me laugh. I liked boys who had an edge to them. I was a bit of a tough nut, into netball and always in a gang. Boys were always secondary to my friends and my social life, so they had to be quite ballsy to get my attention. And once they got me, they had to keep up with me.

Rachael and I double-dated two friends, Paul and Lawrence. They were nice boys and for a while we did everything together – we would go camping and they would take us out on the back of their scramblers. But it was a fickle world – you could be snogging someone's face off on a Friday then flirting with someone else by Monday.

Back then, the place to be was Lysaght's. It was a pub with a hall upstairs where they held a disco every Wednesday night, 7pm till 10pm. There was a time when my whole week revolved around this place. On a Saturday, Mum would take me to the Cattle Market where they sold the best clothes because they were so cheap. If I was lucky she would buy me a whole outfit and it would be hung up on the outside of my wardrobe for the next four days, ready for my next trip to Lysaght's. I had a ra-ra skirt and electric-blue ankle boots with fringing on them. We would crimp or flick our hair, then dance all night, scanning the room for boys we fancied.

I can't remember what I'd done, but one of the few times I was grounded Mum banned me from Lysaght's for a week. I sat looking out of my bedroom window, watching all the other kids on my street heading off to the disco without me. It was pure torture!

There was another teen night at a pub called The King's. It was fortnightly and everyone would get tipsy before turning up in their little groups for a dance. On one night out there a boy kept looking over and smiling. He was tall – already touching six foot, so I knew he must be older than me. His hair was dark and long on top, styled in a side parting with the fringe flicked over one eye and the back shaved into his neck. He was with a group of mates and just from the way he held himself I could tell he was fun. I grabbed Rachael and shouted in her ear over the music. 'See that boy over there? Go and ask him if he likes me.'

His name was Ian, he was sixteen and two years above me at Hartridge High School, just over a mile away from Lliswerry. He cracked a few jokes and, from the twinkle in his eye, I could feel the spark of something exciting.

After that night, Ian and I would make excuses to hang about close to each other's school, hoping we would bump into each other. After a few casual meetings in the safety of our gangs, we broke away on our own and started to get to know each other properly.

Ian's parents were separated. He lived with his mum in a maisonette in Ringland, Newport, a short bus ride from me, and was close to finishing school and starting work at a local steelworks. Before long we were seeing each other three or four times a week. Sometimes we would socialise in a group, sometimes we would disappear off fishing together so we could be alone. We couldn't get enough of each other. *This is it!* I thought gleefully. I felt like my future was in the bag.

Ian was still friendly with his father and would meet him most Saturdays, so I started tagging along too. Ian would meet me off the bus and the three of us would go for a fry-up at The Georgian. After school in the week I would catch the bus to his so we could sit side by side and watch TV or listen to music. Ian's mum was lovely and always delighted to see me. She loved to bake so I'd always have a cake or something with custard waiting for me. Her creations were usually delicious but one time she put poppy seeds in something and it was vile. I was way too polite to say anything, though.

When Ian started his job at Gwent Steel, as it was called back then, I realised what a grafter he was. He worked five shifts a week and would either be there for six o'clock in the morning or finishing at ten at night. Once he had a full-time wage coming in he was always very generous with his money. During our first summer together we were looking round the shops hand in hand and he bought me an engagement ring for £50 from Ratners. It wasn't an official tell-your-family-and-throw-a-party kind of engagement. I don't think we told anyone apart from a few close mates who teased us about the ring. But it was a very romantic gesture, nonetheless. I was a real magpie who loved jewellery and liked to wear a ring on every finger. I remember lusting after sovereign rings for months and for our first Christmas Ian surprised me with one. It cost him £109 and when I wore it I thought I was so cool.

With money in his pocket, Ian, now 17, became a regular at the pubs on a Friday and Saturday night. In the early days, he would see me on the last bus home then go off to the clubs without me, leaving me green with envy. Occasionally I'd slip him a couple of quid out of my own pocket so he could have a pint on me.

Ian was a regular at The Friendship Pub. It was right by the bus stop so I could go with him for a few hours and still get home on time. A group of us would go up there and play cards. It was there I met Jamie, one of Ian's friends from school, and his girlfriend Jayne who would go on to be a really close friend of mine. When it was time for me to catch the bus, I would kiss Ian goodbye and head home, leaving him to enjoy himself. I remember getting to my stop and always being torn between the longer route home that was well lit, or the shortcut that was dark and dodgy. Well, being the chancer I am, I always took the short cut. I would leg it as fast as I could down the lane, past the odd drunk staggering about at kicking-out time. I would arrive home, cheeks flushed, heart pounding, just in time for bed.

As well as liking a drink and a laugh, Ian was a big fan of the football. It never interested me, so I was happy for him to go off to a match with his mates on a Saturday. They were a smart bunch in their Burberry shirts and Farah trousers, but there would nearly always be a scrap after the game. Once, Ian had his two front teeth knocked out. When I saw him I just shook my head and rolled my eyes.

'Is this football rubbish really worth it?' I laughed.

I left school at 16 and took jobs answering the phones at a local bailiff's office. I didn't plan on being there for ever, but I liked the work and the independence it gave me. And now I was that bit older with some cash coming in, occasionally I was able to join Ian and his mates in the clubs. It was so exciting going from drinking cider in the park to the bright lights of an actual nightclub. There was Tiffany's and Stowaway. I remember the music, the lights, being part of an older crowd – it was exhilarating and I could see why Ian liked it so much. Sadly, it started to become apparent that he liked it all a bit *too* much.

Ian came to develop a real 'work hard, play hard' mentality. When he wasn't at work he was hitting the town hard or at the football with his mates getting into some kind of scrape. It's fun at first, when someone's the life and soul of the party and the one with all the best stories. But when you realise they don't know when to stop, it starts to become a bit tiresome. Ian started going out without me, kicking things off after work on a Friday and not reappearing until Sunday. I liked a good time but he was taking it to the next level. I felt a bit left out and neglected – not to mention worried – and it caused a few arguments. One night he stood me up.

'What happened?' I asked when he finally reappeared.

'I went to Giovanni's for dinner.'

It seemed fishy that Ian and his mates would be eating out at a nice Italian restaurant, so I quizzed him about what he'd had to eat there. Mum rang Giovanni's for me and it didn't take long for us to establish that whatever he said he'd eaten that night wasn't even on the menu. 'You're a bloody liar!' I screamed.

We were on and off for a while and, by the time I turned 18 in February 1990, we were on a break. Mum always spoilt me on my birthday and this year was no different. She bought me a beautiful sovereign necklace to match my ring and cooked a curry for me and a few mates. There was no Rachael this year. She was in a serious relationship and we were drifting apart. Instead, it was me and my friends Alex, Zoe and Joanne, and Tracey, a friend from work. We ate around four o'clock then headed into town to start drinking.

By then I was working full-time as a check-out girl at Tesco. I had no set career plan. I was all about getting set up so I could enjoy life. I made sure I had enough to pay my weekly bill for the clothes I had out of Mum's catalogue and the rest was beer money.

We'd been separated a few months when I bumped into Ian in town one night. He looked good and obviously thought the same about me as he was soon turning on the charm, doing his best to get a smile out of me.

'I've missed you,' he said. 'We should give things another go.'

I liked him too much to put up much of a fight and we were soon picking up where we left off. It was shortly after we rekindled our relationship that I realised my period was late. I confided in a female colleague who suggested we take a urine sample to the chemist to check I wasn't pregnant. It seemed highly unlikely, but I agreed we should rule it out and we hopped on the bus to Ringland shops. Nerves suddenly jangling, I made her take the sample in for me. I sat outside, eyes clamped on the door of the chemist anxiously waiting for her to come back. I don't know why I was so worried. Never in a million years did I think *I* could be expecting a baby. But when she came back out and nodded at me, her face said it all. *Oh right,* I thought, in stunned silence. *I'm having a baby, am I?* It was a very strange piece of news for a girl my age to digest. I mean, I didn't just shrug my shoulders and head off to the pub. I was old enough and bright enough to know this was a big deal, that my life had suddenly spun around and started off in a different direction. And yet I was too young to even begin to comprehend the enormity of a baby – a fact some might say is a blessing of being a young mum.

The first person I rang was my sister, Nat. We agreed that Mum was going to hit the roof so, instead of telling her myself, I rang Dad and asked him to tell her for me. Dad and I were still in touch, even though he had no contact with Mum at this point. It must have been a double shit sandwich for Mum to get a phone call like that, not only from her ex but to tell her that her teenage daughter was making exactly the same mistake she had. Naturally, as soon as she heard the news she was straight on the phone to me.

'What's this about you being bloody pregnant?' she snapped.

My defensive teenage response was something along the lines of, 'Yeah, and … ?'

Mum's gut reaction was that I should get rid of the baby and she called in reinforcements in the form of Jayne, who had just become a mum herself. I was lying in bed at home when Jayne appeared. In a frantic whisper before Mum followed her in, she said, 'Everything I say to you now, your mother told me to say!'

That morning Mum basically read me the riot act about how my life was over. Jayne sat perched on my bed nodding along, saying, 'You're not going to have any life. You won't be able to go out. Look at me!' The whole thing was comical because I knew full well she was still out drinking all the time.

I can see now that Mum just wanted me to have a life and experience all the things she didn't feel able to. I think that's why she never stopped me going out and having fun. Up until this point, I'd been living the life she never had.

'It's all right for the blokes,' she said. 'They get to go off down the pub. It's the women who get left holding the baby.'

But her words of warning just washed over me. There was never any question in my mind – I wanted to have the baby.

Chapter Two

In hindsight, given how much he liked a drink, Ian wasn't exactly what you would call father material. I can't remember his reaction to the news he was going to be a dad, which makes me think it wasn't particularly good or bad. He wasn't horrified and he wasn't crying tears of joy either, it was probably just somewhere in between. Maybe deep down he already knew a child wasn't going to have too much impact on his life.

With the bombshell that she was going to be a grandma at 37 still sinking in, poor Mum had to face telling Grancha I was pregnant, knowing first-hand how crushed and disappointed he'd be. I can only imagine how tough that conversation was for them both. They can't have been happy about my decision but whatever words they might have had behind closed doors were never said when I was around. To my face, my grandparents, Mum and Colin – who I now considered my step-dad even though they never married – were nothing but practical and supportive.

'You need to think about where you're going to live,' Mum said. 'You know I'll help out as much as I can but there isn't enough room for a baby here.'

Mum was right. The room Nat and I shared was barely big enough for us, let alone a baby and every other thing that goes with it. While I set about looking for somewhere to live, Ian managed to make a sticky situation even worse by getting into trouble with the police. He was arrested for fighting at a football match and given a two-month prison sentence at a young offenders' unit in Usk. This wasn't ideal and did little to endear Ian to my family, but I knew he wasn't a bad lad. This type of thing was fairly typical of almost all the boys I knew.

I visited Ian pretty much every week, sometimes with his mum, sometimes by myself. I told him I had found a shared house to rent on Walsall Street. I moved in right away and we agreed he would join me once he was let out. More than anything, I wanted to prove to my family that I was a grown-up who could stand on her own two feet. Mum let me get on with it, no doubt knowing that I would always need her, even if I liked to act like I didn't.

Still working the tills at Tesco, I never quite settled into my new life at the house on Walsall Street. The guy who lived beneath me gave me the creeps so Mum's sister, Auntie Romaine, took pity on me and let me stay with her for a while. Then Jackie, a friend at Tesco who was also expecting a baby, offered me and Ian a room at her place.

'It's a double room upstairs,' she said. 'We could do with the money so you'd be doing us a huge favour.'

Jackie was a couple of years older than me. She lived with her boyfriend John on Castle Street, just round the corner from my godmother Mary – a real salt-of-the-earth character who had been friends with my mum since they were teenagers. Jackie and John slept in a bedroom on the ground floor. The spare room was plenty big enough for me and Ian, and the four of us would share the rest of the living space. It seemed like the perfect set-up. Ian was released after serving around six weeks of his sentence, and we were delighted to move in and have a chance to get settled before the baby arrived.

Jackie was a very slender girl who watched her weight, even while she was pregnant. She had the neatest little bump and didn't seem to change anywhere else. I, on the other hand, ballooned to the size of a bungalow. Christmas 1990 I was waddling around like a prize turkey. Mum bought me a beautiful bright-pink duffle coat and I was pleased as punch until I realised I couldn't do the bloody thing up.

I took maternity leave from Tesco around eight weeks before I was due and became a full-time Jabba the Hutt. I would make Ian's sandwiches for work the night before purely so I could lie in the next morning. Every single day I would roll out of bed around 10am and watch Richard and Judy with a big bowl of cereal, two pieces of toast and four chocolate biscuits. Later on, I'd waddle to the corner shop and buy a toffee apple then walk home chomping away, literally like a pig with an apple in its mouth. I'd had zero booze the whole time I was pregnant and the one time I tried to smoke a cigarette it made me sick. Food was my only friend and I ate everything except the carpet.

With the baby due in 11 days, my 19th birthday on 10 February was painfully low key. We had a family meal at Mum's then went to the pub up the road where I drank lemonade and felt enormous.

On 20 February, the day before my due date, I had a driving lesson to keep busy. Almost as soon as I got home, there was a knock at the door. It was Mum.

'What you doing out of work?' I asked.

'Ian's had an accident. You need to come with me.'

That morning – the day before our baby was due – Ian suffered a terrible accident at work. Two large steel coils weighing six tonnes each had fallen right on top of him, breaking his femur and shattering his pelvis. He was initially taken to Newport Hospital, but his injuries were so bad he was quickly transferred to Cardiff, where he had access to more specialist treatment.

Clueless to how bad the situation was, Mum and I jumped in a taxi and made our way to Cardiff Hospital to find out what had gone on. Ian's parents were already there. He was awake but moaning and groaning, still in a huge amount of pain. Although his injuries were hidden under hospital blankets, the doctors told his mum and dad the damage was so bad that Ian's broken bones were now like a jigsaw puzzle. He was incredibly lucky to be alive.

For the next few days I was backwards and forwards to the hospital spending as much time as I could at Ian's bedside. I was probably there as much as – if not more than – his parents, just doing what I felt a good girlfriend should be doing. He was awake but in a fair bit of pain. We were warned that he would be in hospital for several weeks, healing then undergoing physio. This meant that I was going to be having a baby without him, but our impending arrival was kind of pushed to the back of everyone's mind. There was a lot going on, but as I was so young the severity of it all went over my head.

Very early in the morning on 26 February, I woke up with what felt like period pains. I went downstairs and made a cuppa, and when Jackie and John got up I told them what was going on.

'I'm getting these pains,' I said, rubbing my bump.

'Shall I take you to the hospital?' John asked.

'Hold on,' Jackie said, 'let's time how far apart the pains arc.'

After a short while, we realised that the pain was coming in waves every two minutes.

'Call an ambulance!' Jackie cried. 'This baby's on the way!'

In truc Rachel style, me and my huge bump made our grand entrance at Newport Hospital in an ambulance. The pain kept coming but it was nothing I couldn't handle. *This is easy!* I thought, settling down in a hospital bed and picking up the phone to ring my mother.

'Guess where I am,' I said smugly. 'I'm in labour in the hospital!'

'No, you're not,' Mum said. I sounded so jovial she thought I was winding her up.

'I am!' I assured her. 'Everything's fine, don't rush. All these girls on the ward screaming their heads off, I don't know what the fuss is about!'

Twelve hours later it was a whole different story. With Mum and Jayne by my side for moral support, I was screaming in pain, chugging on the gas and air like nobody's business. I got through so many bottles of gas. They weren't all full but I remember the midwife changing it four or five times. My lips were dry and cracked from constantly sucking on the plastic tube. If I'd known what an epidural was I would have begged for one. We tried a shot of pethidine in my leg but it did nothing for the pain. I looked and felt like death. I remember Ian's dad coming in to check on me at one point, but he didn't stick around.

'This is the worst pain ever!' I cried to Mum. 'It's so bad. If I could kill myself I would.'

I had quite a young student midwife called Adele who encouraged me to push before I was fully dilated. I pushed so hard that I burst all the blood vessels under my eyes. The baby was back to back – the wrong position for a natural birth, and notoriously painful for the mother.

The whole ordeal lasted 16 agonising hours. Thankfully, at 7pm on 26 February, the pain was finally over. Out popped a chunky little baby, blinking at the lights. The relief was immense.

'Oh my God,' Mum gasped. 'It's a boy! Look at his hair!'

He was 8lb 11oz with a shock of black hair and the absolute image of Ian. The midwife wrapped him in a towel and handed him to me. I looked down at his scrunchy little face and just couldn't believe he was mine.

Ian was a big U2 fan and had suggested the name Joshua because he loved their album *The Joshua Tree*. When our baby arrived, he looked just like a Josh. It was perfect. Mum took the first photograph and promised to get a copy printed off for Ian.

I needed stitches and was kept in hospital for three or four days. I remember waddling to the canteen one day and bumping into a girl from Tesco.

'Oh, hiya, love!' she said, glancing down at my belly. 'I thought you'd had the baby?'

'I have,' I said, suddenly feeling painfully self-conscious. *This baby weight has got to go,* I thought.

Once I was discharged I went straight back to Jackie's house on Castle Street. I could have stayed at Mum's for a few days but I was stubborn and still trying to prove a point. She did take a week off work though. She would turn up every morning to check on me and help nurse the baby so I could take a shower or have a tidy up. I told her I wanted to lose weight so she would make me a healthy cooked breakfast, just like the ones she had when she did Slimming World. When she wasn't around I reverted to more unhealthy tactics, skipping meals to smoke a cigarette instead.

Josh was around a week old when I took him to Cardiff Royal Infirmary to meet his father. Doctors had warned Ian that his recovery was going to be a very long and slow process. Jayne and Jamie very kindly offered me a lift to save me getting the bus. It was an emotional moment, turning up at Ian's bedside with his son. He'd just had an operation, but was still able to shuffle himself upright and cuddle Josh for a while. He had the first photograph of me holding Josh on his bedside cabinet, stuck up with toothpaste because that's all he had.

'As soon as I saw that picture,' Ian said proudly, 'I had no doubt whose son he is!'

When Josh was a couple of weeks old, Ian called me from the hospital and asked me to marry him. I don't know if it was a knee-jerk reaction, or if he suddenly had the fear of losing me or never finding anyone else, but until that moment it wasn't even remotely on my radar. It didn't feel 100 per cent right, but we had a baby together and he was in hospital having just survived a near-fatal accident. I suppose I felt I had to say yes.

For seven weeks I took Josh to the hospital on the bus pretty much every afternoon. It was a hell of a bus ride – 45 minutes with a baby in a pram. I don't know how I did it. It was a crazy time for everyone in our house as Jackie had given birth to a little girl, Aleysha, just ten days after I had Josh. It was great to have Jackie around as she knew exactly what I was going through. Her and John were always offering to help, asking if I needed anything from the shops. Mum was amazing too and Natalie would come and stay with me most weekends. But with all the sleepless nights and long bus journeys, I started to feel burnt out very quickly. Things were so full on I really struggled to bond with Josh in those precious early weeks. I was coming to terms with being a first-time mum pretty much singlehandedly, while dealing with the fallout from Ian's accident at the same time. I didn't realise just how much we had on our plates. I was just on autopilot, getting through each day.

One afternoon I was sat in the chair next to Ian's bed, trying desperately to wind Josh after a feed, when he projectile vomited. It literally shot out of him and travelled about six feet.

I can't do this any more, I thought, fighting back tears. *I'm so exhausted.*

Ian did show an interest in all the mundane chat about feeding and nappy changing, but *he* was the patient. There never seemed to be much sympathy for me being ripped to shreds in childbirth and left to cope alone.

We clung on for the day Ian was allowed home, when we could be together in one place without the long stressful bus ride between us. But in reality, once he was discharged and dropped off by his dad with crutches and a wheelchair, we faced a whole new set of problems. The house was nowhere near equipped to deal with his needs. For example, he couldn't get upstairs so had no choice but to sleep downstairs in the living room we shared with Jackie and John. I am not joking when I say it was like having two babies. Ian would have to shout up to me if he needed the loo in the night, and when the sofa became unbearable for him I would have to carry him upstairs to bed. I took to placing one of the baby monitors next to him so I would hear him if he needed me. All this as well as getting up to feed and settle a baby every two hours. During the day there were hospital and physio appointments. Ian's mum tried to help out, as did Jackie and John, but I was physically and emotionally drained.

Tension built up and we started bickering. Ian was frustrated about being on bed rest and I was pushed to my limits being mother, father, housewife and nurse. Jackie and John tried to go about their lives as normal, but there was no escaping the stressful atmosphere.

The only thing I could think of to help the situation was to get us out of the house more. Nat would come over and watch Josh for me and I would take Ian out in his wheelchair to get some fresh air. He was a lot heavier than me though, so it was really hard work. The wheelchair was very unforgiving so poor Ian felt every bump in the road and whenever I tried to get him up and down kerbs he would almost tip out.

The silver lining in all this was that we were quickly bumped up the council housing list on medical grounds and landed ourselves a lovely two-up, two-down terrace on Magor Street. It was very close to Black Ash Park and still close to my family. Our parents helped us move in and it felt so good to have a family home – our own space and much more of it!

Slowly but surely, after a few months at home Ian was back on his feet. He received a large compensation pay out from work – something like £100,000 – which to us felt like winning the lottery. Sensibly, Ian didn't get all the money in a lump sum. Instead, he requested interim payments to help us get by, which meant a cheque for five thousand here and another five thousand there. Most of it went on day-to-day stuff, like food and things we needed for Josh, but we did have a cheeky blowout in Cardiff one day where we both got rigged out with a load of new clothes. I felt like I'd earned it. Naturally, Ian had a few blowouts of his own down the pub with his mates. *He's bound to want to let off steam,* I thought. *He's been cooped up for months.*

We started planning the wedding – a service at St John's on Chepstow Road and a party at the Lawn Club, which was cheap and slap bang opposite the church. Mum paid for the wedding breakfast and cobbled together another £500 for my dress. It was a frothy meringue with a huge bow. I laugh about it now, but at the time I thought I looked an absolute dream. I asked Nat, Ian's sister Suzanne, Tracey from Tesco and my two cousins Emma and Sian to be bridesmaids, while best-man duties went to Jayne's husband, Jamie. I got in touch with my dad and asked him to give me away, but Mum wasn't happy.

'It's nothing to do with him,' she said snappily.

'He's my father!' I said. I appreciated she might not want her ex there now she was so happy with Colin but, whatever had gone on in the past, I wanted my dad to walk me down the aisle.

After a very tacky hen night with more plastic penises than I care to remember, the wedding was finally upon us. The morning of 25 July 1992, as I stood waiting for the wedding car to arrive, I felt sick with nerves – not about the wedding itself, but about whether I was doing the right thing. I remember turning to Alex and whispering: 'I give this six months.' She thought I was joking, but I wasn't.

During his speech, Ian presented me with a gold necklace. That evening with the disco in full swing, everyone commented on how pretty it was and how beautifully it caught the light. It was a great party and Ian was on top form. As I watched him enjoying himself all dressed up in his suit, I hoped the wedding would be a turning point for us – the start of a new chapter and the chance to be a regular family. But, sadly, it was the beginning of the end.

In the weeks after the wedding Ian's appetite for alcohol returned with a vengeance. He never went back to work, so with compensation money in the bank and time on his hands he started spending more and more time at the pub. Mum's words of warning kept bouncing around in my head: 'It's all right for the blokes – it's the women who get stuck at home with the kids.' How right she was. Some weekends it was just like the old days – out on Friday, home on Sunday. Ian was drinking heavily, gambling, going to the football with the boys and getting into fights or off raving in a field somewhere. There were rumours he'd been kissing other girls and I suspected he might have been taking drugs. If I tried to challenge him, he would shrug it off and deny everything. We had a child now and we were married. I started to resent being the only one taking our responsibilities seriously.

'If this is the life you want,' I warned, 'go and live it. But it's not the life I want.'

In the end, my marriage to Ian didn't last anywhere close to six months. Just seven weeks after the wedding I told him it was over. He packed his things and went back to his mum's. A couple of weeks later, when the reality had finally sunk in, he called and begged me to take him back.

'It's too little, too late,' I said. 'You're never going to change. I want a divorce.'

Chapter Three

No one wants to be a divorcee at the age of 20, but I wasn't one to sit around crying into a tub of ice cream. Compared to looking after, worrying about, and arguing with Ian, life as a single mum felt like a breeze. Having quality time alone with Josh meant I was finally bonding with him the way I wanted to and being able to stay in the council property on Magor Street gave us the security we needed.

I loved taking care of the house and kept to a strict cleaning routine. Every morning I would hoover and polish the house from top to bottom, rewarding myself afterwards with a coffee and a cigarette. I was so busy keeping house and looking after Josh I would usually skip lunch and maybe even dinner, pausing briefly to puff away on a calorie-free fag instead. The baby weight was soon a distant memory.

Josh was 18 months old now and one of those kids who was perfectly happy in his own little world. You could plonk him in the play pen and he'd sit and play with his cars for hours. He was daft as a brush and dopey as anything. If there was something to trip over he'd trip over it. If there was something to spill he'd spill it. But as long as he was fed and watered, he was very little trouble.

Once the dust settled between me and Ian, he did the right thing and said that even if we couldn't be together he still wanted to be a part of Josh's life. I wanted Josh to have a relationship with his father so we agreed that Ian would pick him up on Saturday mornings and spend the day with him.

Mum and my step-dad Colin idolised Josh because he was their first grandchild and they'd never had a little boy around. They helped us out a lot back then. In February 1993, when I turned 21 and became a fully fledged adult, instead of buying me the usual mountain of presents they decorated my living room for me. It desperately needed doing so I was very grateful, but I was so used to being spoilt that I'm ashamed to say part of me couldn't help but feel cheated out of my gifts!

Despite no longer sharing their house, I still kept in contact with my old housemates Jackie and John. As luck would have it, they ended up moving to Magor Street just a few doors down from me. I was over the moon because Josh could play with their little girl, Aleysha, and with my good mate Zoe just round the corner on Dudley Street, I felt like I was surrounded by good friends as well as making new ones.

Lisa at number 92 was an acquaintance of Jackie and John's. We realised that I had been at her wedding reception because her husband was friends with Ian. Lisa was a few years older than me but we got on like a house on fire and thought nothing of turning up on each other's doorstep whenever we felt like it. Lisa didn't talk about her family much, but she was the third of five children and one day when I popped round her eldest brother Darren was there. I recognised him from Lisa's wedding – a whopping six foot seven tall and 18 stone of solid muscle, he had stuck out like a sore thumb. Now I was seeing him up close, it was even harder not to stare. I'd seen men as broad and muscly but never so tall with it.

Darren was 26 and lived in a flat on Malpas Road right next to a cemetery. He started renting it off their other sister Rachael when she moved in with her fella but didn't want to sell up. Darren had a girlfriend and had recently started working as a doorman at the weekend. Given the size of him it was hardly surprising to hear he was a bouncer. He was obviously a tough guy, but seemed like a bit of a softy underneath and really good fun. I knew if he was anything like Lisa we were bound to get along.

A little while after meeting Darren, I heard that he had split up with his girlfriend. I didn't know the details but he seemed to be round at Lisa's a lot more after that. One afternoon when I was round there, Darren took his top off in front of me. Well, I didn't know where to look!

'Take a picture of my back, will you,' he said to Lisa's husband. 'I've been working out and I want to see how all the muscle definition is coming along.'

He flashed me a cheeky grin and I felt my cheeks turn pink. As if someone had flicked a switch, I was suddenly aware of the sparks flying. Taking his top off was cheesy as hell, but it was in that moment that I found myself looking at Darren in a whole new light.

I can't remember who asked who, but on the evening of 9 March 1993 Darren came round to mine so we could chat by ourselves. With Josh, then two, tucked up in bed, we talked and talked like I'd never talked to anyone.

'I saw you at Lisa's wedding,' he said.

'Yeah, my ex knows her husband.'

'Oh, was that your ex you were with? I thought, *What's she doing with him?*'

'Ian's all right.' I shrugged. 'It just didn't work out.'

'When I saw you that night, I thought you looked just like Demi Moore.'

'Everyone says that,' I laughed. 'I bloody wish!'

'I used to be a right skinny bugger, you know,' Darren laughed.

'Never!' I replied, open-mouthed. It seemed ludicrous looking at the man-mountain before me.

'God's honest truth!' He nodded. 'I was a lanky streak of piss. I ate like a horse but could never put on weight.'

'Worse problems to have!'

'Not for a teenage boy,' he shrugged. 'Being really tall and really skinny makes you an easy target.'

Darren was a sickly child who had asthma, eczema and suffered terrible bullying at school. He told me that before he started working out he weighed around 12 stone, which at his height of six foot seven must have looked dreadful. It was no wonder he went to the gym and took so much care over his appearance.

On top of the daily abuse from the kids at school, Darren had a terrible time at home. He said his father Jimmy – who also worked as a bouncer in Newport town centre – not only cheated on Darren's mother whenever he felt like it, but beat her on a regular basis even when the kids were around. This was quite shocking to me. I was a tough nut who had seen my fair share of scraps, but I'd never experienced systematic abuse and certainly not at home. I thought back to the slap that ended Mum and Ray's marriage and felt grateful I had never witnessed anything more than that. As the eldest, Darren had often ushered his brother and sisters out of the house so they wouldn't have to see or hear their mother being attacked. One particularly bad time, it was dark so Darren knotted a load of bedsheets together so he could get them all out of harm's way and march them safely through the woods to their nanna's house on the Brynglas Estate.

'My God,' I said. 'That's horrific. Why didn't your mum leave?'

'They've been together since they were kids,' Darren explained. 'She was always getting injunctions out against him but she would always take him back.'

My heart went out to him as he told me how his dad would ridicule him for being skinny and call him gay because he didn't get a girlfriend until he was 19.

'I just didn't have a clue how to talk to girls,' he explained.

He had several half-brothers and -sisters on account of his father's infidelity. Worst of all, Darren's brother Wayne, who was less than a year younger than him, had killed himself. The suicide in 1989, just four years before Darren and I met, had been a huge shock to the whole family.

'We had no idea,' Darren said. 'Mum had run away to Tenby to get away from Dad. I went out there to see her and he just did it. I wish he'd talked to me. I wish I could have done something.'

We talked and talked until we realised it was getting light outside. I looked at the time; it was six o'clock in the morning!

'I should probably be making a move,' Darren smiled. 'But I'd really like to do this again sometime.'

'Me too,' I replied.

That night really felt like the start of something special. Darren had opened up to me about so many personal things that I couldn't help but feel close to him. *Does he fancy me?* I wondered, butterflies leaping around my stomach. I knew one thing for sure: I couldn't wait to see him again.

Chapter Four

Darren went to the gym in the evenings and worked the door at weekends, which meant he had lots of free time during the week. To my delight, he turned up for coffee a few times then asked if he could take me and Josh out for the day.

'OK,' I smiled. 'That would be lovely.'

'Great,' he said, looking pleased as punch. 'I'll pick you up tomorrow.'

I had the laugh of my life when I saw his car. He pulled up outside my house in a bright-yellow Mini Metro. Well, you can just imagine how comical a man of his size looked in a car that tiny. I burst out laughing. It looked like he'd sat on the seat and they'd built the car around him.

'All right, Noddy?' I laughed.

I can't recall exactly what we did the very first time Darren took us out because we packed so much in those first few weeks of getting to know each other. It was still only March, but the weather was exceptionally warm for the time of year. We had lots of long drives with the windows down, lovely walks and picnics with Josh in the sunshine. On one walk we came across a little gang of squirrels. Josh was absolutely fascinated and Darren managed to capture a brilliant photograph of us feeding them.

I wasn't quite sure if we were boyfriend and girlfriend yet but with all the time we were spending together it certainly felt that way. With only a few months between breaking up with Ian and meeting Darren I hadn't really had time to think about how being a single mum would affect my personal life. But the way Darren included Josh made me think that he was happy to accept that side of my life as part of the package. I wouldn't say Darren was a natural, but seeing him make an effort was probably one of the things that made me like him. Josh, meanwhile, was so chilled that he was happy to hang out with anyone as long as I was there.

I have a very vivid memory of a day Darren and I spent on our own, hiking up a mountain. I was wearing dungarees with a T-shirt underneath. He was in his tracksuit bottoms and picked me a bunch of wild flowers on the way up. We were laughing and joking the whole time. Darren had me in fits of giggles with his silly jokes and impressions of people. He was a brilliant mimic. At one point I climbed up onto his back for a piggyback ride. I felt so small with my arms wrapped around his huge shoulders and, when he put me down, he had me doubled up in hysterics as he pretended to try to climb on *my* back.

'You look beautiful when you laugh,' he said, pulling me close for a kiss.

After all the stress with Ian I'd had no intention of getting into another relationship. Yet here I was being completely swept off my feet. It was unexpected and exciting. Every time we said goodbye I couldn't wait to see him again.

While things were blossoming with Darren, Ian continued to look after Josh on a Saturday as we agreed. However, it didn't take long for me to cotton on that pretty much all they were doing was sitting in the pub all day. Josh was either playing with the balls on the pool table or just sat with a bag of crisps from behind the bar, and I was far from happy about it.

'If you think the pub is an acceptable way to spend the day with a toddler, then you're an even bigger idiot than I thought,' I snapped.

Our contact with Ian fizzled out very quickly after that. I think Darren was pleased. He didn't seem to like me speaking to Ian very much, which was understandable. No one likes an ex hanging round. It was a real shame for Josh, but I counted my blessings that he was still too young to really notice his dad was no longer around.

Darren worked the door at two venues in the centre of Newport. He would be at the Penn and Wig – which used to be The Georgian – until closing time, then he would move on to the nightclub Zanzibar, which was where I used to party when it was the Stowaway. I can understand how some women would hate their boyfriend being in that environment. Bouncers are out late at night and surrounded by drink and drugs. The women are dressed up to the nines and the men are all looking for a fight. But Darren was so good to me and seemed so honest and genuine that I had no worries about any of that. He was clearly big enough to look after himself so I never feared for his safety. And he was so disgusted by his father's infidelity that it seemed highly unlikely he would stray.

'You're such a natural beauty,' Darren would say. 'Not like those girls up town with their fake hair and fake eyelashes. They're like Easter eggs – take the wrapping off and they're just cheap, plain chocolate underneath.'

Everything Darren said and did made me feel like he was serious about me. He had no qualms about introducing me to his parents, taking me for a drink at the King's Hotel where his mum Barbara worked as a barmaid. His mum and dad were separated, but Darren always felt certain that something was still going on between them and, lo and behold, we bumped into Jimmy at the bar having a couple of pints before his shift on the door.

They were both bouncers, and both blessed in the height department, but the similarities between Darren and his father seemed to end there. Jimmy liked a drink, unlike Darren, who took his fitness so seriously that he only allowed himself a couple at the weekend. Again, this was very attractive to me. After all the problems caused by Ian's partying it was a relief to be with someone who had no interest whatsoever in that lifestyle. The only downside to being with such a health-conscious man was that he didn't like me smoking. He hated the smell so I naturally found myself cutting down, which – let's face it – was no bad thing.

When my friend Alex threw a house party a couple of months into our relationship, I knew it wasn't Darren's thing but desperately wanted him to come and meet everyone.

'It's her twenty-first birthday!' I said. 'Come on, it'll be fun!'

After a lot of arm twisting he agreed. We left Josh round at my mum's for the night and walked to the party via Black Ash Park. We had a great time – Darren was on form and all my mates seemed to like him. But once we said our goodbyes and started off on our own, his mood changed.

'So what about you then, you little slag?' he spat.

'Eh?' I replied, unsure whether he was joking or not.

'How many boyfriends you had before me then?'

After a brief moment, I remembered a conversation we'd had at the party. An ex of mine had been mentioned, completely innocently and in passing. He wasn't even really a proper boyfriend, just someone I'd been on a few nights out with.

That must be why he's upset, I thought.

'It wasn't anything serious,' I said, trying to reassure him, even though he was clearly overreacting. 'It's history. It's nothing to do with you and me.'

The next thing I knew I had lost my footing and was toppling down a small embankment. I landed awkwardly, face down in a bed of stinging nettles. *Did Darren just push me?* I thought, struggling to my feet. I climbed back up to the footpath expecting Darren to hold out a hand and help me up, but he was already walking away. Tipsy, confused and with my face stinging like mad, all I could do was follow him like a wounded puppy.

When we got back to my place I hurried inside, grabbed some of Josh's Sudacrem and plastered it all over my face. It was the only thing I could think of that might relieve the stings. I took a few deep breaths and collected my thoughts. *What the hell just happened? He's never spoken to me like that before. And did he really just push me over?*

'Look what you've done!' I said, turning to him and pointing to my face. I expected an apology, an explanation – something. But he couldn't even look at me. He went straight back out the door, got in his Mini Metro and left. I went to bed with my face still throbbing. I felt so upset that we'd had our first argument that I cried myself to sleep.

When I woke up the next morning I was still struggling to make sense of what happened. I was hurt and angry because I felt sure Darren had pushed me down the bank in a temper, but I was also confused. I didn't see how the mention of someone irrelevant from my past was grounds to react in that way. I was also baffled by the way Darren walked out on me once I got home. I wanted to know what was going on in his head. *Does he want to break up with me?* I wondered. It seemed a shame to throw away something that had been so good up until now.

I'd not been out of bed long when Darren turned up at the house. I was glad – I didn't want to play silly games, I wanted to sort this out. The second he clapped eyes on me he broke down.

'My God, Rachel,' he said. 'I'm so sorry. Are you OK?'

I nodded sternly. I wanted Darren to know I was mad at him, but inside I couldn't help but be taken aback by how upset he was.

'I can't believe I did that to you,' he said, sinking his head into his hands. 'I didn't mean to do it. It was an accident.'

'It didn't feel like an accident,' I said. 'Was it because of what you heard at the party?'

'You're right,' he said, wiping his nose. 'I was jealous. I was jealous and I shoved you. But I swear I didn't mean to push you so hard. I didn't know you were going to fall like that. I'm so sorry, Rachel.'

He was sobbing uncontrollably now. He was a wreck.

'OK, calm down,' I said, walking over to him.

'I was jealous,' he said between sobs. 'Jealous because I'm in love with you. I love you, Rachel. I was jealous because I love you so much.'

I put my arms around him and he cried into my belly like a baby. I'd never seen a man cry, let alone a man like Darren.

'Why didn't you help me up?' I asked. 'You didn't even say sorry or ask if I was OK.'

'I know,' he said. 'I'm sorry. I scared myself. I was embarrassed. The second I pushed you I just wanted to undo what I'd done.'

I felt myself softening. It was hard to be mad at a man who was crying his eyes out with remorse.

His tear-stained face was looking up at me now. 'It won't happen again, Rachel, I promise you. It won't happen again. Ever.'

I looked into his eyes and saw the sad little boy he'd told me about. It seemed plausible that he'd pushed me in the heat of the moment without realising his own strength. *We all get jealous sometimes,* I thought. *My God, he's so upset … It wasn't even that bad!*

I hugged him close.

'Next time, can we just talk about it?' I asked.

'Yes, my love,' he said, nodding. 'I promise.'

Chapter Five

After the incident in Black Ash Park, Darren went out of his way to make it up to me. He came round almost every day and was nothing but sweet, loving and attentive. He was always asking if I was OK and checking if I needed anything. I'd never known a man work so hard for my affections. *I could get used to this!* I thought. The way he behaved and made me feel was so like a fairy tale I almost forgot our fight at the park ever happened.

Darren did take me out for dinner once or twice, but we didn't have much money between us, so he would usually come to mine where I would cook for him. He loved my cooking, and over dinner he liked to talk about the future, about where we would live one day, and the type of house we'd have. Darren always said he couldn't wait to be a dad because his father had done such a good job of showing him what not to do.

Although I missed Darren a lot when he was out at work at the weekends, part of me enjoyed my Friday and Saturday nights without him. It felt healthy for us to have some space. Occasionally, Mum and Colin would have Josh for me so I could go out with Alex. We definitely had at least one night out when Darren was on the door, but I kept my distance because he was working.

I was surviving week to week on benefits so for a bit of extra money, me, Alex, her sister Lianne and Darren's sister Lisa went down to Twickenham to sell raffle tickets at the rugby. We hung around outside the grounds selling tickets to people going in and got paid cash in hand when we were done. It was pretty fun, but afterwards Darren admitted he had hated it.

'I know what the rugby boys are like,' he said.

'You've got absolutely nothing to worry about,' I said, looking up at him as I wrapped my arms around his waist. And I really meant it. I was a loyal girlfriend and I didn't want anybody else. Darren told me I was the most beautiful girl in the world. He made me feel safe, secure and protected, and when he opened up to me about his past and his grief for his brother, Wayne, I saw his vulnerable side. I wanted to support and protect him too.

As we grew closer, I came to understand just how deep the scars from Darren's childhood ran. I remember him acting strangely one day, as if he couldn't keep still, and he told me he was having a panic attack.

'I'll be OK in a minute,' he said.

Darren had battled depression and anxiety for most of his life and had been on a combination of antidepressants and anxiety medication for years. When I found out that it was Darren's tablets Wayne had used to end his life, my heart just broke for him. It was no wonder he carried so much guilt and anger. Although they were all still in touch, Darren hated his father for the violence and infidelity, and despised his mother for always taking him back. In Darren's mind, his parents were responsible not only for Wayne's suicide, but for the damage to his own mental health as well. 'They've got a lot to answer for,' he'd say darkly.

Darren hung onto his flat and kept his name on the housing list just in case, but spent nearly every night at mine. We had a lot of deep chats about his family, about starting our own and working towards buying a bigger house. I loved falling asleep on his chest and making him his coffee in the mornings. I even knocked the smoking on the head as a show of my commitment to him and our future.

'You're such a great mum,' he'd say. 'I can't wait for you to have my babies. Look at your perfect face … just imagine how beautiful they'll be.'

Everything about our relationship felt right. We just wanted to support and take care of each other. In my eyes, Darren was The One and he couldn't tell me enough that he felt the same about me.

I was 22 and had been with Darren just over a year when I missed a period. When a pregnancy test came up positive, we were giddy with excitement.

'I'm going to be the best dad ever,' Darren whispered, giving me one of his bear hugs.

Sadly, our excitement was short-lived. Seven weeks into the pregnancy, I started bleeding. The doctor confirmed I had miscarried and ordered me home to bed. Darren's uncle was getting married that weekend and we were supposed to be going to the wedding.

'I can't go now,' I told him. 'The doctor says I need to rest. And I don't really feel up to it.'

I assumed Darren would stay at mine and look after me, but he put on his suit and went to the wedding without me. I tried not to feel too hurt. *I guess there's not much he can do,* I thought. *And it* is *his uncle's wedding.*

I fell pregnant again very quickly after that. Darren came to all the appointments and took a great interest in my health and the baby's development. Again, this was very different to my experience with Ian, who could never come to the midwife because he was always at work.

I was very excited about the fact that Josh was going to be a big brother. To be honest, I was probably more excited about it than Josh! He was three now and had such a funny and quirk little personality. Occasionally, I would wonder if he might be missing out by not seeing his real dad. But the face Darren pulled if Ian ever came up in conversation made me think it was best to let sleeping dogs lie.

I still spoke to Mum on the phone every other day and really wanted to tell her about the baby, but I didn't have a good feeling about it. She had met Darren one night when a few of us were round at a family friend's watching a Mike Tyson fight. Darren came to pick me up and ended up staying for a beer. He got a bit loud and obnoxious, bragging that he'd compared measurements and was actually bigger than Tyson. I glanced nervously at Mum, who was watching Darren with a look of disdain on her face. She never said a word but I could tell she wasn't impressed. After that night, I couldn't shake the feeling that she didn't like him. Mum and Colin were still very much part of my and Josh's lives. Mum worked full-time at a local solicitor's office, so I saw them mostly on weekends, which meant my relationship with Darren felt very separate. I didn't feel he had been fully accepted into the family fold yet, but hoped that in time they would get to see the side of him I fell in love with.

In the end, I did the same thing I did when I fell pregnant with Josh: I got someone else to tell Mum for me. My sister Nat was still living at home so I decided the best approach was to tell her I was pregnant and get her to tell Mum. It was a bit of a cop out really because I still had to face Mum once she knew. And just as I expected, she wasn't thrilled.

'I can't believe this, Rachel,' she said. 'You haven't known Darren long.'

'I know, but I never wanted Josh to be an only child. I want him to have a brother or sister.'

'But it's so soon. Why couldn't you just wait a bit?'

She had a point, but I was young and headstrong. As far as I was concerned, I knew everything about Darren. We had been together for a whole year – it didn't feel like we were rushing anything. I didn't value Mum's advice as much as I should have done, and anyway, there was no way I was getting rid of the baby now.

Although he had been staying at Magor Street most nights, Darren moved in officially at the end of 1994. With a baby on the way it seemed like the perfect time to take that step. The plan was to live there together temporarily while saving up to buy somewhere bigger a bit further down the line. I was still managing on benefits while Darren was earning cash in hand for his work as a doorman. Because he wasn't officially on the books, he claimed dole on the side as well. I told him I didn't feel right about that, but he insisted he'd done it for years with no comeback and made me feel daft for worrying.

Ever since leaving home I'd been a stickler for budgeting my money. I liked to know exactly what my outgoings were for the week and how much I had left to spend. When Darren moved in he was quite happy to put our money in one pot and let me take charge of it. I knew I would do a good job of keeping our finances in check and felt good that he trusted me to do that.

I'd always known Darren was a creature of habit, but living with him and seeing it first-hand was really quite something. He went to the gym five evenings a week: no ifs or buts or maybes. He worked the door Friday and Saturday nights, then spent Sundays hunting with his mates. Darren owned a few working dogs – Patterdale and Lakeland terriers which were kept at his mother's house – and every Sunday he would get up at the crack of dawn and take them out to some farmland to hunt. I knew very little about hunting at the time, but I knew it was something close to Darren's heart, as he had taken up the hobby with his brother, Wayne. The dogs were trained to hunt foxes and catch badgers using a process called 'digging'. The men dug tunnels deep into the ground, put tracking collars on the dogs, then sent them down to catch and kill whatever they found. The men would then have to dig ditches some five and six feet deep to get to the badgers that the dogs had trapped inside. It was brutal – not to mention illegal – but Darren said the farmers were grateful because it helped stop the spread of tuberculosis.

Some of the possessions Darren brought with him when he moved into my house were books on gangsters, hunting knives and the heads of a dead fox and a badger.

'What the bloody hell are they?' I asked as he pulled the heads out of a cardboard box.

'Trophies,' he said proudly. 'I thought we could put them up here, on this wall.'

I thought they were vile, but let him hang them up to keep him happy. This was now *our* house, after all. Darren's mate built some kennels at the bottom of my garden so the dogs could move in too. Nat and I had never been allowed pets as kids so I quite liked the idea of it.

My pregnancy was going really well. Everyone said I was glowing and I kept busy by being super organised, getting all the baby's things washed and ready. At night, I would put Josh to bed then cook Darren a healthy meal ready for when he got home from the gym. Afterwards, we would lie cuddled up in bed, feeling the baby kick and mulling over names we liked. You couldn't find out the sex of the baby back then, so we made sure we kept our options open. We agreed Jack or William were nice strong names for a boy and we loved Demi for a girl. I had absolutely no nerves about becoming a mum again and I think a lot of it was down to how stable I felt with Darren. Despite the odd petty squabble, Darren said and did all the right things and my pregnancy was a really happy, exciting time in our relationship.

Sadly, two months before the birth all that changed. It was during the day and Josh was out at nursery. I can't remember what the argument was about but it very quickly spiralled out of control. Voices were raised and I stormed off upstairs to cool down. Darren followed me up to our bedroom, unable to drop whatever it was we were fighting about. In a rage, I turned to face him but before I could speak he had his hands around my throat. I tried desperately to prise his giant fingers off me, but they didn't budge. He squeezed tighter and pulled upwards. I felt my feet lift up off the ground. I was choking for air and squirming, barely able to make a sound. It went on for what seemed like for ever. Then just as the room went dark, he let go.

Darren slumped down onto the bed, put his head in his hands and started to cry. Still coughing and spluttering, I stayed on the floor for a few moments, soothing my neck with my fingers as I tried to steady my breathing. My ears were ringing; blood and adrenalin were whooshing desperately through my veins. When I felt able to stand, I staggered to my feet and took myself downstairs to get a glass of water. It didn't take long for Darren to follow, his face red and puffy with tears.

'I can't believe you just did that,' I said quietly. My voice was raspy and it was quite painful to speak.

'Me too,' he said. 'I'm so sorry. Are you OK?'

'I'm fine.'

'Your lips went blue. I was so scared I'd hurt you. Is the baby OK? I don't know what got into me.'

We were both in complete shock. Neither of us could believe what he'd done, not just to me but to the baby.

If you ask a woman what she would do after an incident like that, they all say they would run for the hills. But I was struggling to join the dots. The Darren I knew was golden, not the man in the bedroom with his hands around my throat. And the second it was over he was broken, tearful, remorseful and utterly devastated by his actions.

'Please don't leave me,' he begged. 'Not now, not over this. You and the baby mean everything to me. I can't lose you both now.'

The look in Darren's eyes was pure fear and I knew exactly why he was so scared. His first girlfriend had dumped him and slept with someone else. The situation left him so heartbroken that he'd come close to taking his own life. He went as far as throwing a hose in the back of his car and driving somewhere secluded. Although he never went through with it, he had to spend time in a hospital psychiatric ward before he could get over it all.

Darren clearly had a lot of very complex issues, but I was 22 and we were in deep with a baby on the way. It was very hard to admit to myself that I might be having another child in a relationship that might not be ready for one. So, in the days after our fight, while Darren fussed over me with endless cups of tea, the easiest thing to do was chalk it up as a blip. He needed me and I didn't want to be on my own with Josh and a new baby. We were going to work at what we'd got.

'It will never happen again,' he promised. 'I adore you. I need you. You're the strongest person I know.'

Everyone thought he was this big tough guy and yet, ironically, I felt it was my strength and love that held him together.

Chapter Six

To my Darling Rachel,
As long as you're in my life I'm strong,
I'm whole, I'm everything
Happy Birthday babe,
Love you forever
Darren
xxxxxxx

In February 1995, I turned 23, then began packing hospital bags and mentally preparing myself for birth number two. The baby was getting heavier by the day and nearly every woman who saw me waddling around gave me advice on how best to trigger labour. By March, I was so fed up that I was ready and willing to try every single one of the old wives' tales. Someone told me that castor oil helps stimulate the womb so I bought some, stuck a tablespoon of it into a large glass of orange juice, held my nose and chugged it down. It was 8 March – the day before the anniversary of when Darren and I got together. That evening we invited his sister Lisa round and the three of us ordered ourselves a spicy curry – another favourite for ladies about to pop. We also watched *Terminator* because, apparently, a jumpy film can help too.

I don't know if it was the oil, the curry or Arnold Schwarzenegger, but at some point during the movie I felt a sharp twinge.

'I think I might have just had a contraction,' I said.

Darren sprang to life, calling Mum as we'd arranged so she could come and get Josh for us.

She came straight over and scooped the little man out of bed as Darren loaded my bags into the boot of the Mini Metro. Mum carried Josh to hers and settled him in bed there. At some point, she left Colin in charge and got a taxi to the hospital. I don't recall whether I'd asked her to be present at the birth or whether she came to check on me and ended up staying, but either way I was glad to see her.

Darren was busy revelling in the limelight of being the expectant father. We had a giggle in the labour suite as he had his picture taken with a stethoscope, pretending to listen to my bump. But when lunchtime hit and his tummy rumbled, he shot straight off to the canteen. Nothing got in the way of Darren and his food. Mum decided to go with him, leaving me to be assessed by a junior midwife. There was some concern that the baby might have the umbilical cord wrapped around its neck, so she decided she was going to break my waters for me to help things along. I was still so traumatised by the pain I experienced delivering Josh that, when she asked if I would like an epidural, I almost bit her hand off. She gave me the drugs to dull the contractions, only for me to start feeling desperate for a wee.

'I really need to go,' I said.

'But you shouldn't be able to feel it,' she said.

'Well, I'm telling you, I can feel it and I really need to go!'

The midwife quickly hooked me up to a catheter and I filled two bags in about two minutes flat.

By the time Mum and Darren came back to the room I was so relaxed from the epidural that I was drifting in and out of sleep. Just before 4pm, I really felt like I wanted to push. The midwife had another look downstairs and to her surprise I was already fully dilated.

'If you feel the urge to push again, just go with it,' she said.

Darren was stood at the end of the bed watching the whole thing in a kind of horrified silence. I remember him slowly edging backwards.

'You'll be going through the wall in a minute, Da!' I quipped.

By 4.10pm the baby was out. The midwife had barely had time to get her gloves on. The cord was wrapped around the baby's neck, just like we had feared. She cut it quickly and a load of liquid squirted her in the face and went all up the curtains.

It was a boy weighing 9 pounds 2 ounces, born on 9 March 1995 – two years to the day Darren and I had got together. We called him Jack. Darren was absolutely over the moon to have a son and really loved the significance of the date.

'Our anniversary,' he said, kissing my forehead. 'It was meant to be.'

'He looks exactly like Josh did!' Mum said proudly.

Once we were settled, Mum got ready to go home and see to Josh.

'Give the big brother my love, will you, Mum,' I said.

'Of course, love,' she said. 'I'll bring him up tomorrow.'

She left and I sighed with contentment as I looked down at the tiny baby in my arms.

And then the bubble burst.

'Who the fuck does she think she is?' Darren snapped.

'You what?' I said.

'Your fucking mother. Saying my son looks like Josh, like that ugly fucking ex-boyfriend of yours? How fucking dare she.'

He was absolutely raging.

'What are you on about, Da?' I said. 'It was just a flippant comment! Calm down! I've just had a baby, for fuck's sake!'

He stormed out, his face crimson with anger. I felt tears prick my eyes then drop down my cheeks as I looked down at Jack, asleep in my arms. *How could he be so vile when I'd just delivered a baby? Wasn't he happy? Wasn't he proud of us?*

I stood up carefully and shuffled to the window that was looking down on the car park. I saw Darren marching to his car. When he glanced up, I waved. He stuck two fingers up at me and drove away.

I spent two nights in hospital after the birth. I was told I was free to go home after one, but I point-blank refused. Although the labour had been much easier with the epidural, I was still incredibly tired and just didn't feel ready. Maybe subconsciously it was a way of avoiding Darren after his nasty outburst, but it didn't register at the time. I don't remember him apologising for the vicious things he said about my mother, but he was back at my bedside the next day, holding Jack proudly and playing the dutiful father as visitors came and went. Mum and Colin brought Josh to see me. We sat him down and placed Jack in his lap for a photo. We asked what he thought of his new baby brother but he didn't say a word. He just sat there with a huge dopey grin on his face, looking down at Jack then back up at me.

When I finally got home, I was still exhausted. I thought I'd be a pro the second time around, but I'd forgotten how tough the combination of labour and a newborn was. I thought that, because Darren only worked two nights a week on the door, he would be free to help with the night feeds and I could catch up on some sleep. But after just one night, the shrill sound of a baby crying was too much for Darren and he moved himself into Josh's room. With my hormones still all over the place I couldn't help but feel crushed. *It'll just be for a couple of nights,* I hoped.

Jack was a very hungry baby who seemed to cry whenever I put him down. It was like he wanted to be close to me all the time. Those first few weeks of trying to juggle a difficult baby and a four-year-old while trying to run a house to my standards were a blur of broken sleep and strong coffee.

Despite all the reassuring things he'd said to me when I was pregnant, about how he was going to be a hands-on dad, Darren didn't seem very engaged with the baby. He certainly didn't seem interested in helping with Josh or picking up any of the slack around the house. I realised I was watching Darren go about his life as if nothing had changed. He never missed a single session at the gym. Every Friday and Saturday night he worked the door and every Sunday, as long as the weather was right, he went out with the dogs. When he *was* at home, he seemed more likely to pick up a book about the Kray twins than to pick up his son. We started to bicker a lot. Every night I hoped he'd get into bed with me to smooth things over with a talk and a cuddle, and every night he bunked up in Josh's room.

'I need my sleep, love,' he'd say, 'or I won't have enough energy to train.'

I tried to be understanding because I knew how important the gym was for his self-esteem, but for three long months I slept alone, getting up to feed the baby when he cried. In the dead of night when I was sat by myself trying to settle Jack, again I heard my mother's warning: 'It's all right for the blokes. It's the women who get left with the kids.'

I wasn't happy and I wasn't going to stand for it – not again. With the resentment building up inside me I started to moan at Darren about getting a proper job.

'We're a family now,' I told him. 'We need a full-time wage coming in.'

'Join the rat race?' he scoffed. 'No fucking way. It's a mug's game.'

But with me stuck at home looking after two children he didn't have a leg to stand on, especially if we were ever going to buy this dream house he wanted. Every day I nagged and put the pressure on. I made suggestions and looked in the paper for work that would suit him. I wasn't going to stand for a man who didn't pull his weight when he had a family to support. If he couldn't help around the house, he was bloody well going out to work.

I was like a dog with a bone and I pushed and pushed until Darren snapped. He grabbed a radio with both hands, lifted it above his head and smashed it onto the floor. Shocked, I backed away to avoid the debris, but he reached out with his right fist and pulled me back towards him by my hair. My legs buckled.

'Ow!' I screamed. 'Get off! You're hurting me!'

'Just shut the fuck up!' he shouted. 'Stop telling me what to do!'

He dragged me along the floor by my hair, letting out a roar of frustration as he finally released his grip. It was all over in seconds.

I never set out to push Darren that far, but I think by this time I knew him so well that part of me had an idea what was coming. In the seconds before he blew, something told me to brace myself. Then afterwards, as I sat rubbing the back of my head and he slumped down onto the sofa with tears in his eyes, I knew he would be sorry and willing to do anything to make it up to me.

Sure enough, as well as a grovelling apology and a bunch of flowers, Darren agreed to get a job. I thought I'd finally got my way, but sadly Darren's idea of looking for work was very different to everyone else's. He had no intention of getting down the job centre or dusting off a suit for interviews. Instead, he came up with a way of emptying the pound coins out of fruit machines.

'You do realise that's robbery,' I told him.

'It's easy money, babe,' he said. 'Easy money, low risk.'

I really wasn't happy but nothing I said made any difference. In Darren's eyes, I'd been nagging him because we were skint and he'd come up with a solution to the problem. He had a device that mimicked a pound coin going into the slot of the gambler and he worked out roughly how many times he had to do it before the machine paid out the jackpot. The tool Darren used was small and fiddly to make. He had hands like shovels and zero patience so at one point he talked me into making more of them for him. He could be very persuasive when he wanted to be. All I got out of it was the embarrassment of paying for my food shop with one-pound coins. This was a world away from the proper job I'd been pushing for, but the money he stole paid the bills and kept food on the table. I just had to live with it and hope it was temporary.

Despite managing to stay off the fags, I had no trouble losing the baby weight after Jack. He was a real handful who seemed to need my attention 24 hours a day. I was so flat out cleaning, cooking and looking after two kids that I barely had time to eat. Occasionally, when Josh was at nursery I would stick Jack in the pushchair and walk into town for some exercise. He was three or four months old and I was pushing him along Corporation Road when Darren happened to drive past us. He turned the yellow Metro around and pulled up alongside me. I thought he was just going to say hello but as soon as I clocked his face I knew otherwise.

'Where are you fucking going?' he spat through his window.

'I'm just walking into town.'

'Why aren't you getting the bus?'

'It's easier to walk with the pushchair.'

I was suddenly aware of how busy it was around us.

'You know what, Rachel? You're a fucking slag!'

He was shouting now, on a busy main road teeming with cars and pedestrians. I felt so embarrassed. It must have been obvious to everyone we were arguing. I hated that he was causing a scene in public, and I could not for the life of me understand what I'd done wrong.

Darren drove off in a rage, engine revving and tyres screeching. I did my shopping then walked back to the house, knowing Darren would be there feeling terrible for the way he spoke to me.

'I don't want you out walking like that again,' he said. 'What if it rains? You shouldn't be struggling with Jack and the shopping. And anyone could be beeping their horns at you, I ain't having it.'

The penny dropped: I was looking good and the thought of another man checking me out in the street absolutely tore him up inside.

'I'm getting you a car,' he went on, 'just a little run-around. I'll feel better knowing you're safe.'

I didn't like the way he behaved when he was jealous but I certainly understood it. *He knows what men are like,* I thought.

A week later, Darren presented me with a little navy-blue Fiesta. I was very grateful. I had passed my driving test when I was 20 and still with Ian. My first car – a gold Talbot Horizon we bought using £350 of his compensation money from the steelworks – had long since gone to the knacker's yard.

Sadly, the Fiesta came with a side helping of drama. It had belonged to Darren's mum but, when he asked if he could take it off her hands and give it to me, he found out she'd already sold it to someone else in the family. Darren managed to buy it back, but then discovered that loads of unnecessary work had been done to it.

'We've been fucking ripped off,' he fumed.

Nothing was ever straightforward where Darren was concerned. I was always having to calm him down and reassure him. Everything he did seemed to be more hassle than it was worth. And unfortunately, buying me a car didn't stop him from getting jealous. He still preferred to drive me around himself, if he could

He was taking me to the Post Office to get my family allowance when things kicked off again. I got out of the car and could hear someone beeping. I daren't look. Knowing Darren's eyes were on me I would never acknowledge anything like that just in case it was a random bloke or some workmen. But it didn't stop. It went on for so long that in the end I had to turn my head and see who it was. Lo and behold, it was someone we knew – Tom, the boyfriend of Colin's niece Julie. We waved at each other then he pulled out and drove away. Just as I feared, Darren was getting out of his car and shouting obscenities at the driver. While Tom disappeared up the road oblivious to the furore, I scurried into the Post Office to the sound of Darren shouting, 'I'll smash your face in, you fucker!'

I stood in the queue to collect my allowance, dreading going back outside. I left the shop and walked back to the car where Darren was still fuming.

'I took his reg, I'll find him and smash his fucking head in beeping at you like that.'

'Darren,' I said, 'it was Tom, Julie's boyfriend.'

His face dropped.

'Oh, was it?' he said. 'Oh right … that's all right then.'

He'd made such a fool of himself it was almost laughable. I was glad Josh was at nursery and it was only Jack in the car as he was still little enough for Darren's language to go over his head.

With Jack's first Christmas coming up, I was looking forward to having dinner at home, just the four of us. It had always been such a special time for me growing up that I had lots of grand ideas about how it would be now I had Darren and a little family of my own. As a parent, you look forward to the children being excited and all the little traditions you're going to have. Darren seemed to be looking forward to it too, although he told me he had quite a strict routine for Christmas morning. He liked to meet his family for a drink, then they would all go to the cemetery together and lay a wreath on Wayne's grave. I could see how important this was to him, so we agreed that I would do Christmas dinner for 1.30pm – plenty of time for him to do what he needed to do then get back home to eat. But when the time came me and the boys were sat at the table waiting and Darren didn't show. Two o'clock came, then half past. I was worried the dinner would spoil so Josh and I tucked in, and I gave Jack a little bit of everything on the tray of his high chair. By the time Darren walked through the door we were almost finished.

'Everything all right, love?' I asked.

'Yeah.'

'I thought we said dinner at half one?'

'Didn't realise the time.'

He spent the rest of the day looking miserable as I fussed over the kids to try to lift the mood. I felt dejected that he hadn't rushed home to be with us on Christmas Day, but given the circumstances – that he had been visiting his brother's grave – I put it down to grief.

I really wished that Darren would spend more one-on-one time with Jack. I thought it would be good for both of them, but whenever I brought it up Darren always had an excuse. One of the few times I managed to talk him into watching Jack for me, I got back from the supermarket less than an hour later thinking he might have enjoyed some father–son time, but he just thrust Jack into my arms the second I walked through the door.

'Here,' he grunted. 'You deal with him.'

I hadn't even finished bringing the shopping in.

Looking back, I think Darren was really insecure about his ability to be a father. After all, he hadn't had the greatest example in his own dad. In Darren's eyes, children were women's work.

I started to realise that there were greater depths to his jealousy, too. Because of his ex, Darren was deeply paranoid that I was going to leave him for someone else. Once, after a row, I went for a walk to clear my head and, when I came back, Darren had thrown a plate of baked beans up the wall.

'Why you done that for?' I asked.

'I thought you'd left me,' he said sheepishly.

It was so ridiculous and Darren felt so embarrassed for assuming the worst of me that he sulked around the house like a wounded animal for the rest of the day.

'The best thing you can do is find yourself a new fucking boyfriend,' he said.

He was clearly fishing for more reassurance, but having just scrubbed a load of baked beans off the wall I wasn't in the mood to give it to him. Without thinking, I said sarcastically, 'Yeah? Maybe I already have.'

I knew I shouldn't have said those words before I'd even finished saying them. Darren was not someone who could make light of a sentence like that.

I felt the cool breeze on my face before I could process what had happened. Darren had booted the front door so hard it had come off its hinges and was dangling by the chain. Standing there looking at the damage he'd done, it didn't take long for Darren to see the stupidity of his actions. What were we supposed to do without a front door? He got straight on the phone to his dad and asked him to come over and help fix it. Darren wanted to repair the damage he'd done, not just to the door but to my opinion of him. He was hot-headed one minute, desperate to redeem himself the next. I put up with this merry-go-round because I knew he had issues. When he was good he was golden and for all his faults he absolutely worshipped the ground I walked on.

Chapter Seven

Darren always said I was the only person he had ever opened up to and that he would never dream of keeping anything from me. He was one of those people who believed everyone was entitled to the truth. One night we were lying in bed having one of our chats when he suddenly went quiet on me.

'What's wrong?' I asked.

'I've got something to tell you,' he said. 'Ray's not your father.'

Darren's mother played on a women's baseball team with my godmother Mary. Anyway, somehow the story that Ray wasn't my real dad had come up in conversation and Darren's mum passed on what she heard to him. I didn't remember a time when Ray wasn't around, but apparently, when I was roughly four years old, before Mum and Ray had Natalie, he adopted me.

As you can imagine, this came as quite a shock, although it suddenly made sense of the fact that Natalie and I look absolutely nothing alike. I wouldn't say I was devastated to be hearing all this from Darren, but I definitely had a lot to think about. *Should I tell my mother I know? Do I want to find my real dad?* If it was true, it was no wonder Mum had been so funny about me asking Ray to give me away at my wedding to Ian!

After a short period of time getting my head around this new information, I decided to go to the local births, deaths and marriages office to see a copy of my birth certificate for myself. A very petite lady looked it up for me, then sat me down and confirmed that I had in fact been adopted.

'Oh God,' I said. 'Please tell me my mum is my mum and my nanna Dolly is my nanna Dolly.'

'Yes, all that is correct,' she said. 'But Ray is your adoptive father, not your biological father.'

The crazy thing is, if I'd been asked for my birth certificate when I married Ian, I would have found out years earlier.

Darren felt very strongly that I should confront my mother and demand the truth about who my dad was.

'You deserve to know,' he said.

I was blind to it at the time, but he was painting himself as the hero. He knew my mother didn't like him so this was all a great opportunity to stir up trouble for her.

With Darren constantly in my ear, I spent weeks avoiding the subject with Mum. It felt like Pandora's Box and I wasn't sure I wanted to open it. But it simmered away inside me and the next time she was on her high horse picking holes in my parenting (as she often liked to do) it came out.

'Oh, by the way,' I said. 'Who's my father then?'

It was a real *EastEnders* moment. You could almost hear the drums.

'Oh, Rachel,' she said. 'I'm sorry.'

'Why didn't you tell me?'

'I always planned to, but it never seemed like the right time. I thought I'd tell you when you were ten, then when you were sixteen. But I could never do it. The more I put it off the harder it was.'

Seeing her anguish, I could totally appreciate the dilemma she was in. She only ever wanted to try to do the right thing.

'So who is he?'

'Just some boy. We were so young. He wasn't ready to be a dad. Then Ray came along ...'

I didn't push her any further. I figured that, whoever my real dad was, he must have been a real arsehole to leave Mum on her own like that. I told Natalie what had been going on and she was positively enthralled by the drama.

'Ooh, I wonder who he is!' she exclaimed. 'You know what we should do – we should ask Mary.'

She was right: our godmother Mary was bound to know something, but I wasn't quite ready to ask. I was going to keep the situation under my hat for now.

For Jack's first birthday in March 1996, I decided to throw a little party at Magor Street. Judging by his face when I told him, Darren wasn't very keen on the idea. He seemed to be getting less and less sociable, especially where family were concerned.

'I don't know why you're fucking bothering,' he said grumpily. 'It's not like Jack's going to remember it.'

I dismissed his comments with a roll of my eyes. It was Jack's first birthday and I wanted to celebrate.

The morning of the party I rushed about preparing a spread of buffet food and making sure everything was tidy. Darren chose to keep a low profile rather than offer to help, but this was always his way. His behaviour made it clear to me that there were things in life – like housework and children – that were solely my responsibility.

Mum came along to the party, bringing Nat and Nanna Dolly with her. My cousins Emma and Sian were there and Jayne, who had two girls now – Jodie and Kayleigh – brought them along too. Darren made a half-hearted attempt to mingle, but it didn't come naturally to him. He didn't do well with small talk so I would find myself being even more chatty than usual to compensate for him.

We had a shop bought cake in the shape of a cute dog. When we sang happy birthday, Jack was in his usual spot on my hip. I held the cake in my other hand and encouraged him to blow out the candles. He stared at the cake for a moment then leant forward and sank his teeth right into it.

Now Jack was one, I was so tired of scraping by that I felt I had no choice but to get back to work myself. The fruit-machine manufacturers had got wise to what people like Darren were doing and fitted a new mechanism to stop the machines from being fiddled. I was relieved, thinking maybe this would be the catalyst to Darren finding a regular job, but he never seemed to share my urgency about how we were going to put food on the table.

My next-door neighbour Kim worked at Ashton Park Residential Home and told me they were looking for care workers.

'Do you fancy some shifts?' she asked.

It didn't sound like my kind of thing but I asked her what the care workers did, just to be polite.

'You get the oldies up, get them washed, dressed and fed. Sometimes you have to help bathe them and get them to the toilet.'

'I have enough trouble wiping my own arse never mind someone else's!' I laughed.

'Once you've wiped one arse, Rachel,' she said, 'they're all the same!'

After thinking about it for a few days, I decided to take Kim up on her offer. I did love older people; maybe it would be fun. She arranged for me to work Friday tea times 5pm–9pm and the Sunday night shift 8pm–8am. It was very physical work. You were constantly on your feet, lifting, bending and running about. A few of the residents had dementia, but, although they struggled with their short-term memory, they could still remember all their old stories. This was magical to me and at quiet times during my shifts I loved to sit down and listen to them.

Some of the residents could be quite difficult, like Hettie, who was always getting out of bed and wandering around during the night. She was quite scary-looking – very tall and thin. She had this long grey hair that, after an hour or two tossing and turning in bed, would look wild. I'd be sat in the lounge at 2am, watching telly and listening out for anyone ringing their buzzer for assistance, when I'd hear this big deep voice shout, 'Toast!' She would be stood on the stairs like a ghost, demanding toast and frightening me half to death.

To make ends meet I took a second job working a couple of days a week for a money-lending firm called Shop-a-Cheque. On Mondays, Fridays and sometimes Saturdays, I was a debt collector, knocking on doors and trying to get money out of people. It worked on percentage so the more you collected the better your wage that week. Unfortunately, it was in a really deprived area of Newport where no one had any money. It was a round no one else at the company wanted because they always had their car windows put through. But I knew so many of the families from my school days I figured I'd be all right.

It was out of the question to expect Darren to watch the boys while I was working during the day; I just knew it would be too much to ask of him. Mum and Colin helped as much as they could at weekends and sometimes I'd sling my cousin Emma a fiver to watch the boys for me. Every week felt like I was flying by the seat of my pants and there were times none of my go-to babysitters was available and I would have no choice but to take the kids collecting with me. Josh would sit quietly in the car, no trouble, but Jack would be crawling around all over the place, trying to escape. If he was being a handful, I would take him with me into a client's house. One of the times I did that, he nicked a lighter. I had no idea until I was stood outside the next house, glancing back at the car and caught sight of him trying to light it.

Some of the houses we had to go to were absolutely awful, but none of that fazed me. I was always chatty and pleasant and I certainly didn't judge. One girl, Terry, was notorious for being a bad payer. She wouldn't pay anybody and didn't give a shit about the consequences. One day she let me in, plonked herself on the downstairs loo right in front of me and lit up a fag while she did a wee.

'You got any money for me then, love?' I asked.

'Nah, love.'

'Come on, Terry, you must have something, even if it's just 50p.'

She would never pay anyone else but she would always give me something, even if it was just the bare minimum. I was terrible, though – I couldn't stand to see people get in a mess, so if someone couldn't pay I'd chuck 50 pence of my own money in to keep them out of bad debt. Darren knew I did it. 'I'd do the same,' he'd say. He was just as soft as me. We felt too sorry for people. It was the wrong job for me, really. But no one ever touched my windows.

It felt good to keep busy and have money coming in, but I started to wonder if there was something better out there for me, something more long term. One day I bumped into a lady called Frances. She was one of my nicer Shop-a-Cheque customers and knew Darren's family. She asked how work was going and I told her I wanted something with a bit more potential.

'Why don't you do hairdressing?' she said. 'You'd be great at it! And it's something you can always earn money from.'

She was right – I'd always loved hair and make-up. Maybe this was the career for me. I heard there were courses going at Nash College so I drove down there and picked up some leaflets. I could do hairdressing levels one and two over two years and only have to attend college for one full day a week. I knew I could ask Mum to have the boys for me so I signed up as soon as I could.

Chapter Eight

> To My Darling Rachel
> *You are my one true Valentine*
> *The one I will always love*
> *You were meant for me so please please please*
> *Always be my Valentine*
> *In this life and the next*
> *Love u*
> *Always*
> *Darren*

Staggering out of the taxi, I rummaged around in my handbag for my key while trying to stifle a drunken giggle. I'd been for staff drinks with Kim and the other girls from the nursing home. It had been a lifetime since my last night out and I'd gone along wanting to let my hair down.

As I'd got myself ready earlier that night, Darren didn't try to stop me going but certainly made his feelings known.

'You're not wearing that, are you?' he'd said when he saw my outfit. 'Get those fake eyelashes off. You don't fucking need them.'

He was such a grump about it I wondered if it was worth the hassle. *Why am I bothering?* I thought. But then I reminded myself that *he* was allowed to do whatever he wanted. I'd been going to college, looking after the kids and working two jobs. Tonight was my turn.

I tucked the boys into bed then Darren saw me off with a strict curfew. I had to be home by midnight, which I thought was reasonable. I knew things would be winding down by then anyway.

I had a good night: life had been so full on lately that it was great to have a change of scenery and a laugh and a joke over a drink. But it was always in the back of my mind to make sure I was home in a cab five minutes early. I never wanted to give Darren an excuse to pick a fight.

However, once I'd got out of the taxi and hugged Kim goodbye, I couldn't get my key in the lock. My whole body went hot. It was almost midnight and I couldn't be late. I knocked lightly on the door, but he didn't answer. *Shit!* I thought. *What am I going to do?*

In a panic, I knocked Kim's door.

'I'm locked out! Can you ring the house phone for me?'

The phone rang and rang but Darren didn't answer. When he finally realised what was going on, he came to the door and let me in.

'Thank God for that!' I said, relieved. 'I've been stood out here for ten minutes!'

Darren looked sheepish.

'What's the matter with you?' I asked.

He'd been sat waiting up for me all along. He put the latch on so he would know what time I got in and sat himself at the front window getting more and more worked up the closer it got to midnight. Then when he heard the cab pull up he legged it upstairs to pretend he was in bed. On the way up he stubbed his toe and completely forgot that I wouldn't be able to get in.

'I was fuming,' he said. 'When I heard the phone ring I thought the cab couldn't have been you and you were still in town, ringing to say you'd be late.'

He was so stressed out. The whole thing was comical but it didn't stop the guilt.

'It was just a night with the girls,' I said, kissing him. 'I'm home now.'

I still wished Darren would find a proper job and help more with the kids, but those day-to-day niggles seemed to be a common thread for just about every couple I knew. As long as Darren was still head over heels in love with me, I thought we could get through anything. To mark every Christmas, birthday, Valentine's Day and the anniversary of when we got together I always got a card with a long, emotional passage about how beautiful I was and how much I meant to him. I didn't know of any other man who pored over such romantic cards for his partner.

In return I worked hard to be the perfect woman. To get the most out of his body-building, Darren liked to eat clean through the week, so I took care to buy and feed him the things he needed to keep in shape. For breakfast he would have eight Weetabix, for lunch I would do rice and broccoli with either tuna or chicken, and for snacks he would have Muller Rice, bananas and endless boiled eggs. With all the various supplements and protein powders on top, Darren's weight and size only ever seemed to go up and that was exactly how he liked it.

At the weekend, Darren liked to have a blowout which usually involved me buying him a big cream cake of some sort. He had a real sweet tooth and I somehow found time to do a baking course so I could make him homemade cakes just like his mother had.

In August 1996, with Darren's thirtieth birthday coming up, I arranged to have a cake made. I probably could have baked one myself, but I wasn't creative enough with the decorating and as it was a special birthday I wanted him to have the best of the best. To make him laugh, I asked for the cake to have a little body builder on it made of icing. Everything was organised and I was buzzing for his birthday until one afternoon when we were in the house on our own, he started picking a fight. He seemed determined to have a row, goading me with comment after snide comment. He was saying nasty things like, 'you're a lazy fucking bitch', things we both knew weren't true. I bit my tongue, knowing what he was like and that he was probably just having a bad day. But he went on and on until eventually I lost my patience.

'Oh, just shut the fuck up, Darren,' I snapped.

Well, this was like waving a red rag to a bull. He took his chance to strike, grabbing hold of me by the back of my head. I collapsed downward, eyes scrunched in pain and screaming at him to stop as he swung me around the kitchen by my hair. When he was done, he thrust me into a heap like he was tossing rubbish into a bin. My heart was going like the clappers. With adrenalin rushing through me, I leapt to my feet calling him every name under the sun.

'Get the fuck out of my house!' I screamed. 'I don't want you anywhere near me! Get your stuff and go!'

Darren stormed out, slamming the front door behind him so hard it felt like the whole house shook. I was absolutely fuming that after all the tears and promises Darren had got physical with me again. I looked down at the floor and wondered what all the black marks were. Where I'd been struggling the rubber soles of my shoes had left scuff marks everywhere, like dirty tyre marks on a road. *He can stick his bloody birthday,* I thought as I scrubbed the kitchen floor.

Darren must have known I was mad because he didn't show his face for a few days. I assumed he was on the sofa at one of his sisters' and made the most of the chance to calm down without him moping around the house like a child. By this time the routine of Darren losing his temper then making a tearful apology was pretty well worn. I would soon be making excuses for him in my head, trying to explain away the latest outburst. I would always look at what I could have done differently, you know, maybe I shouldn't have said this or that. I would always get back to the same conclusion: that Darren loved me. He was a complicated man who needed a strong woman.

When the time came to pick up the birthday cake I still didn't feel like he deserved it, but thought I might as well get it now I'd paid for it. When I saw the little body builder and his dumbbells I couldn't help but smile. My friend had done such a great job and I knew Darren would love it. I took the cake home and left it on the side, knowing he would soon be turning up at the house with a bunch of flowers. And sure enough, he did.

'I feel terrible,' he said, looking down at the floor in remorse.

'So you should.'

'I just wasn't feeling myself. Maybe it was my nerves, I don't know. But I shouldn't have taken it out on you. I'm sorry.'

'I saw the cake,' he went on. 'I snuck round the back to try to apologise and I saw it through the window. I'm gutted I messed up like this while you were doing that for me. I'm so ashamed of myself. It won't happen again.'

'You keep saying that,' I said.

'I know, but I mean it. You know it's not me. I want to be better.'

I started to wonder if we were just an emotionally charged couple or whether I was experiencing domestic abuse. But I was a strong girl, not some timid wallflower. I wasn't being controlled or beaten up every day; the incidents were few and far between. Plus, I knew Darren inside and out – if he was moody I knew he was thinking about his brother, and if he was snappy I knew it was the anxiety talking. It seemed inconceivable that Darren would grow up with domestic violence then go on to become a perpetrator. And he was always so remorseful when he stepped out of line. I couldn't tell you exactly what constituted an abuser, but I didn't imagine it was a man who wrote love notes and sobbed his heart out after losing his temper. I would joke with him that it was like living with two men: Darren was the bad one and Daniel was good. I guess I felt that if I wanted Daniel I had to put up with Darren from time to time. And I believed I had enough love and strength in me to do that.

Darren had been dabbling in anabolic steroids for years, believing it helped with his weight training. He kept it hidden from me in the early days when he could keep a supply safely stashed away at his own flat. When he moved in with me and Josh he pretended they were vitamins at first, but even when he fessed up I didn't really understand what they were. These days just the *word* 'steroids' sounds scary to people, but we were clueless back then.

'Everyone takes them,' he said. 'It helps with muscle growth and there are no side effects with these ones, they're perfectly safe.'

But in 1997, Darren – who could never keep a secret from me for long – told me that he had started injecting. He was using testosterone and a steroid called Ganabol, which was originally manufactured as a growth hormone for horses. He bought most of his supply from someone at the gym, costing a couple of hundred quid for three months' worth. He had books on steroids which advised him to do three months on and three months off, so that's pretty much what he did. I was shocked by how much these things cost. It seemed a lot of money to be spending when we had two kids to think about, but what did I know about weight training?

We took the boys, aged two and six, to Majorca for a week that year and Darren stumbled across some Ganabol in a chemist. He was over the moon because it was much cheaper than buying it illegally back home. I was in charge of looking after the holiday money and knew exactly how much we had to spend each day. Without even asking if we could afford it, Darren took a chunk of cash off me so he could stock up.

'I don't know why you want to put chemicals in your body,' I said. 'You're big enough.'

The sun brought out terrible acne on his back and I wondered if it was the Ganabol. But we didn't have the Internet back then;

we didn't have smartphones or Google. I had no way of knowing just how dangerous Ganabol could be, especially for someone already on medication for their mental health. All the blokes at the gym were doing it, so Darren wanted to do it. It just became another thing I had to let him get on with. His mind set was always 'bigger is best'.

While I was doing my hairdressing course, Darren decided that he'd had enough of Magor Street and wanted to buy a house. This gave me another glimmer of hope – if he wanted a mortgage he had to get a permanent job. After a few days pondering what kind of work he could do, Darren decided that he wanted to get his Heavy Goods Vehicle licence, just like his brother Wayne had done. I agreed this type of work could be perfect for him and we looked into it together, full of enthusiasm. Then I remembered that this was Darren and he had absolutely no patience. I didn't dare say it aloud for fear of crushing his dream, but the thought of him learning and passing a test seemed like a pretty big mountain to climb. And with it costing around £1,500 for a course of lessons and the test, it was money we couldn't afford to waste.

I agreed to cover the cost with cash I still had left over from my divorce settlement. Darren contacted some HGV instructors and found one he liked the sound of, then after a few months' training he took his first test. Just as I feared, Darren failed. He was fuming and wanted to kill the instructor for putting him in too soon.

'It's fine,' I soothed. 'You can just take the test again.'

It cost us another two or three hundred pounds for extra lessons and to take the test again. The day Darren took test number two I waited anxiously by the front window so I could read his reaction when he got home. Well, his face said it all: he had failed again. I braced myself for the screaming and shouting. He just couldn't handle the frustration of not being able to do something.

Thankfully, after lots of reassurance from me, a few more lessons and a few more hundred quid, it was a case of third time lucky. Darren got his licence and secured his first driving job at a company called Reymead Transport within a couple of weeks. He was over the moon and saw it as a green light that we were ready to press on with our search for a new house. We got a mortgage offer and started looking. Things were suddenly moving very quickly and, secretly, I wasn't sure if I liked it. Darren and I had been together for four years now and I knew him very well. He had a temper and I had very little confidence that he would be able to hold down this new job. I was bricking it about giving up my place on Magor Street and committing to buying a house with him. My gut was clearly trying to tell me something, but I didn't feel able to speak up. Darren was so excited about the prospect of getting our own home I knew he would be crushed if I pulled out now. He got so upset about things I wanted to avoid upsetting him at all costs. The only choice I had was to go along with it all.

We hadn't been house hunting long when a property round the corner from Darren's nanna popped up in the paper.

'We've got to go and see it,' Darren said.

He was very close to his nanna and had many fond memories of her house on the Brynglas Estate. It was on the opposite side of the River Usk to where I had grown up, but I was willing to take a look.

The property on Brynglas Drive was the very first house we viewed and we both fell in love. It was a terrace with a bedroom each for the boys. It was quite old fashioned inside – it needed new blinds and the carpets needed changing – but it was all cosmetic. There was nothing structural that needed doing, we could just move right in. One of the big selling points was that it was right next to Brynglas woods – a lovely spot with terrific views looking out over the Bristol Channel. Darren had played in these woods as a kid and we agreed it would be a great place for him to walk his dogs. I got so swept away imagining the boys running around the lovely big garden that I forgot all about my nerves. *It's a great place to raise the kids,* I thought. We put an offer in immediately and the seller, Sue, accepted, even though she already had a better offer on the table. As luck would have it, Sue was a good friend of Darren's mum so she decided to offer it to us.

'This is it, babe, our dream home!' he said, ecstatic.

Maybe this house is the answer to all my worries, I thought. *Maybe this is the fresh start we need.*

Chapter Nine

To My Darling Lovely Rachel
27 today, 21 when I met you and I'm so glad I did
So happy to share the last 6 birthdays with
someone so pretty, pretty as the most wonderful
place in the world.
You are my star birthday girl and you will always
shine in my heart whatever life brings
Love you
Crazy Darren
xxx

The sale went through quickly with no hiccups which made me feel like it was all meant to be. Sue very kindly gave us a set of keys before we exchanged, which meant I was able to spend a week filling up the car and going back and forth to drop things off, leaving Darren to get all the bigger stuff onto a van.

We officially moved into our new family home on Brynglas Drive in April 1998. It was so peaceful there and Darren was on a real high about buying a house together. To add to the excitement, we had £2000 cash back as part of our mortgage offer. There were so many things I wanted to buy I must have spent it in my head several times over. But instead of using it to buy things we needed for the house – like new carpets and blinds – Darren had other ideas. He arranged to have new kennels built for the dogs. He installed security cameras outside and looked into buying a second-hand Land Rover he'd seen advertised. My feelings on this were not considered, but I decided to bite my tongue. The dogs needed kennels before they could move in with us, so they were a necessity. And it was high time Darren replaced his comical yellow Metro with a vehicle more suited to a family, so I let him go ahead and buy it. We were getting on well and Darren had a stable job; I knew when to pick my battles.

Jack was now three years old and attending nursery. Josh was seven and getting on well at primary school where he seemed to be making lots of friends. I wouldn't say Darren had a bad relationship with the boys, he just wasn't one for family stuff. He was either working or doing his own thing at the gym – a typical Alpha male. I was quite happy taking the boys to see Mum and Colin on my own two or three times a week. Mum referred to us as the urban foxes because we would turn up and eat all her food.

In 1999, I passed my hairdressing course with flying colours, but left college clueless about how I was going to make the transition into employment. Well, it didn't take long for fate to help me out. I bumped into Frances again who said she needed a junior stylist at her salon Bonkerz. To my surprise, she agreed to take me on for a trial. This was a great opportunity at just the right time. When I got home and told Darren my exciting news, he had a few concerns.

'Yeah, you can work there,' he said, 'but I don't want you cutting no men's hair, mind.'

'Why not?'

'Touching another man's hair while they're perving on you? I ain't having that.'

'It's not a barber's, love.' I shrugged. That much was true. However, it was a unisex salon. I had to call Frances and warn her.

'Listen,' I said, 'I can come and work for you but I can't be cutting any men's hair. Darren won't like it.'

Having to make that call was so embarrassing, but Frances knew Darren's family well. She was aware of the problems they'd had over the years – the violence, the mental health issues and Wayne's suicide. Frances understood.

'Don't worry, Rach,' she said. 'It's mostly women anyway. It'll be fine.'

When I walked through the door on my first day, everyone was so kind and welcoming I knew I'd made the right decision to take up the trade. But Darren didn't make it easy for me. In my first two weeks, he turned up at the salon unannounced several times, saying he wanted to see how I was getting on. I hoped it was a phase and he would get used to me working there, but every night he would quiz me about whether any men had been in. I started to suspect his jealous streak was rearing its ugly head again and found myself telling a white lie that the male trainee was gay, just to keep him off my back.

I don't know if it was the salon or what, but I started to feel like Darren's mental state was going downhill. His mood swings seemed to be getting more unpredictable. He was argumentative all the time and waking up in the middle of the night dripping with sweat. He told me that when he lived alone his anxiety levels got so high that he became obsessive about things around the house. He liked to hoover his carpets a certain way, and then wouldn't want them being walked on. He liked to polish all his taps, and then wouldn't be able to stand it if they got a single finger mark on afterwards. As far as I was aware, Darren had never fretted over anything like that since we'd been together,

I think mostly because I ran such a tidy ship. But I did get a glimpse of it when he dropped a few crumbs of Weetabix behind the bin. I would have cleaned them up if they'd been visible to me, but Darren was the only one who knew they were there. And when they were still there two days later he had a go at me.

Knowing how low Darren got when Wayne died and his first girlfriend left him, I felt like maybe I was seeing warning signs of another depressive episode. I decided the best approach was to encourage him to get help before things got any worse.

'Look, Da,' I said, 'these outbursts aren't good for any of us. We need to try to address this.'

He agreed to mention his temper to the doctor and they increased his medication. They also suggested he should try anger-management classes.

'Just try it,' I said, 'for me.'

He went to one session and came back even angrier than when he went.

'What a pile of crap,' he growled.

There had been a kid there sharing a story about how he'd got angry when he locked his keys in his car. Well, Darren thought this was so pathetic that he wanted to smack the guy's head in. I saw the funny side but the irony was completely lost on Darren.

'It's not for me,' he said. 'They wanted me to relax and imagine I was on a beach. I'm not going back to that hippy shit.'

Although he could open up to me when he was in the right frame of mind, Darren never wanted to appear weak to the outside world. He didn't like being told what to do and he didn't like change. In his head, everything had to be a certain way and, if it wasn't, his frustration would explode out of him as anger.

Everyone at Bonkerz liked to experiment with their hair and would always be trying out different cuts and new colours. I longed to join in but knew Darren wouldn't like it. I'd been wearing my dark hair in a short kind of pixie crop for a while, which he loved because everyone said it made me look like Victoria Beckham. I knew that he would hate any attempt to change it. He liked everything the way he liked it, including me. But one day, the temptation got too much and I asked Frances if I could have a tint put on.

'It's only a hint of colour,' I said. 'He probably won't even notice.'

I left the salon feeling like a million dollars and walked home into World War Three. Darren was furious that I had gone against his wishes. He felt I was disobeying him, that I was deliberately trying to antagonise him, that I was doing it purely to get male attention. He couldn't understand why I would want to change something he thought was perfect already. I tried to explain, to stand my ground and make him see that it really wasn't that big of a deal, but he just went on and on until I agreed to get the tint taken out. The next day I went back into work and begged to be put back to my normal colour. It just wasn't worth the grief.

I had been used to getting 'Daniel' most of the time and Darren only some of the time, but the balance was starting to tip the other way. He would get riled up about anything and everything; if someone had cut him up at a roundabout or looked at him funny in the gym he would come stomping home like a bear with a sore head and take it out on me. He thought nothing of throwing his dinner up the wall: one night I narrowly avoided a bowl of steaming hot stew. Where before he would store up his tantrums for when the boys weren't around, he seemed to be caring less and less what they saw. There would always be an apology afterwards, but there would always be a next time.

On top of this, no matter what I said or did to put his mind at ease, Darren's niggles about my working at Bonkerz became borderline obsessive. He added to his list of rules that I could only cut women's hair if I was sure they weren't gay – as if I would be able to tell! He showed up at the salon a few more times, reaching over the reception desk and helping himself to the appointment book, I assume to check none of my customers had male or lesbian-sounding names. I never put a foot wrong, yet he was always trying to catch me out – which was a bit rich for someone who always seemed to be up to no good.

Darren wasn't just a handful at home, he was well known in Newport – everyone knew big Darren off the door – and he was often approached by friends and friends of friends to sort out problems for people. He might be asked to dish out a warning to someone, intimidate a witness, or even beat someone up. I would always hear about it afterwards, either on the grapevine or from Darren himself, who didn't seem to care whether I found out or not. He could always explain it away as something that just needed to be done, but when he was sitting up in bed at night reading books about the Krays, I started to worry that he wanted to live a kind of gangster lifestyle.

'I wish I was around in the fifties and sixties,' he'd say. 'You could get away with a lot more in those days.'

When I went into work I tried to be my usual bright, breezy and outgoing self, but everyone knew that wherever I went Darren wasn't far behind. They were all well aware of his size and reputation. His very presence was so intimidating that whoever I was working with that day would be nervous for the whole shift in case he showed up.

When a man came in needing a haircut and I was the only stylist available, I knew I was going against Darren's wishes but decided I had to be professional.

'It's fine, Frances,' I said. 'It was bound to happen sometime. I'll do it.'

But as I stood there holding the scissors, my hands started to shake. Frances was so worried for my safety that she put us at a station near the back of the shop and ordered three of the trainees to circle around me so if Darren drove past he wouldn't be able to see. No one ever said as much, but I knew every single one of us was on tenterhooks until I'd finished. I hoped to God I never had to go through that again.

I was working at the salon when Robert, one of Darren's friends, called through to reception. With all Darren's dodgy dealings in the back of my mind my first thought was that he had landed himself in hot water with the police, but not this time.

'Rachel? It's Rob. Darren's had an accident. He's fallen on a bar.'

They had been out digging and Darren had fallen backwards onto one of the bars they push into the ground. The way he landed on it, it had almost impaled him up the bum. It sounds comical but it went in quite deep and he had to be pulled off. Luckily for Darren, the farmer who owned the land turned up with a quad bike and got him to help.

'We're going up to Brecon Hospital. Darren said to meet him there.'

'I'm in the middle of a perm,' I said.

Darren must have heard me because he must had the phone off Rob and came on the line.

'I haven't fallen on a fucking thorn bush!' he bellowed angrily.

'I am in the middle of a perm,' I said again, slamming the phone down. With all his behaviour lately, I wasn't in the mood to go running to his aid.

'What's happened?' Fran asked, having heard me on the phone.

'Darren's had an accident. I might have to leave early.'

Fran was a star about it and let me leave as soon as I was ready. Rob rang back to tell me Darren had insisted he was taken to our local hospital in Newport so I could get to him quicker. When I got there he was in a bed waiting to be assessed.

'Oh, Rach, everything went yellow,' he said dramatically. His injury was worse than I'd thought but I still struggled to muster any sympathy. *It's your own stupid fault,* I thought.

'Do my pillows for me,' he said, leaning forward. I rolled my eyes behind his back. He was going to milk this for all it was worth. I leant forward to adjust his pillows for him and my leather jacket swung in his face.

'What the fuck are you doing?' he snapped. 'You're fucking suffocating me!'

He pushed me away and I lost it. All the frustration I'd been bottling up over the last few months came flooding over me and, in a moment of madness, I grabbed his nose with my fingers and twisted it as hard as I could.

Darren let out an almighty 'Oww!' I stepped back in the nick of time, narrowly avoiding his fist as he swung for me. But he was useless in that hospital bed. He was incapacitated and I took advantage – I had the power for a change.

'Get my fucking stuff and take it to my old man's,' he said. 'I've had it with you.'

'I will,' I said, storming out.

I was quite happy leaving Darren there in the hospital. It was a breath of fresh air to go home knowing he wasn't going to burst through the door with a face on at any moment. Me and the boys could go about our daily lives without him throwing his weight around whenever he felt like it.

But it wasn't to last, of course. Darren's sister, Rachael, rang and pleaded with me to go and see him. I took this as a sign he had calmed down and went up to the hospital with a bag of Mars bars he'd requested. There were eight in the packet and he ate six while I was there.

'Sorry for the other day,' he mumbled half-heartedly. 'I'd just come into hospital, I was in pain.'

I didn't welcome his apology with open arms, but now I had Daniel back I knew I might have a better week or so ahead of me at least. It was nice while it lasted, but as soon as he went back to work his stress levels were back up to maximum. As the months went by, he always seemed to be at loggerheads with his manager over something or other. He would come home and I'd be able to tell by his face whether we were getting Darren or Daniel. Some nights he would walk in the door and launch his rucksack at the wall and I'd know I'd be in for it.

Darren never punched or slapped me full force – my face was far too precious to him and, let's face it, a punch from a man Darren's size would have killed me. In hindsight, he was very aware of his strength, which meant the steady increase of violence was actually far more calculated than I would have liked to believe at the time. He liked to get right in my face and butt his forehead against mine. I would grit my teeth and avoid his stare, trying hard not to rise to the bait. He would grab hold of me by clamping a huge hand underneath my jaw then squeeze my face in anger. I felt like he was always testing me, seeing how far he could push me and how much I could take. I always tried to remain strong, because if I cried he would call me a sissy. Then, of course, the second his anger subsided he would always be sorry. There would be tears and apologies. He would say he hated himself and wanted to die, that he was going to talk to his doctor and get all the help. I got to know the cycle by heart. I knew when I could stand up to him and when to be submissive. If the boys were around when things were getting heated I would say whatever I needed to avoid a row. Darren didn't care but I never wanted things to escalate in front of them if I could help it. If they weren't in the house when he started, I would have a go back. Whatever was going on in his head, I wasn't one to take this type of behaviour lying down. Yes, I had a certain amount of sympathy for his background and mental health problems, but if he was simply being a prick I was bloody well going to tell him.

One day, mid-rant, Darren spat right in my face.

'What did you do that for?' I snapped.

'It's better than hitting you,' he scoffed.

I fled to the bathroom to wash my face, thinking, *You dirty fucking bastard*. I hoped it was a one-off – just like I always did about everything.

I thought about leaving but knew Darren would never accept me breaking up with him. I wanted to get far far away, but it felt impossible to do that with two children. And what if I left and he killed himself? I knew how close he had come before, so I stayed. I made excuses for his behaviour and stuck it out. I coped by savouring the peace when he was out working, at the gym or hunting. If I couldn't leave, all I could do was hope that one day maybe things would settle down.

The tension had been brewing for months when Darren and his manager had their final bust-up. It didn't get physical but voices were raised, Darren pushed his luck too far and had to come home and tell me he'd lost his job. Although I half expected it was coming, the worry had me feeling sick for days. Darren was the main earner and, although I looked after all the money, it was his wages that paid the mortgage. Thankfully, he was so happy at Brynglas Drive that he was willing to do anything to not fall behind on the repayments. He organised some driving through an agency and assured me it was just to tide us over while he looked for something more permanent.

The situation about not knowing my real dad still played on my mind from time to time but it was Nat who brought it up again.

I was giving her a driving lesson in my Fiesta when she suddenly had a bright idea.

'Come on, Rach, you'll be thirty soon! Don't you wanna know who he is?'

'Oh I dunno, sis,' I said. 'He's probably a right arsehole.'

'Did you ever ask Mary?' she said.

'Nah, I didn't get round to it.'

'Let's do it now!' she said, slowing down and indicating. 'It's not far from here. Let's do it!'

She was turning round now.

'No, I don't want to!'

'Come on, don't be a wimp.'

'Well, you can ask her then.'

I let Natalie drive us to Mary's and then sent her to knock on the door and do the talking. I had a habit of getting her to do my dirty work.

I sat watching them for a few moments, then they turned to me and beckoned me over. I got out of the car and we all went inside and sat down in Mary's living room.

'Listen, Rach,' she said in her thick Welsh accent. 'You're right. Ray's not your dad but that's all I can really say. I don't want to step on your mum's toes. You need to ask her.'

I couldn't face another showdown with Mum so I sat on it for a few more months. But just like before, it simmered away inside me, ready to explode next time she rubbed me up the wrong way.

'You need to tell me who my father is,' I said.

She put her hands on her hips and took a deep breath. 'Rachel,' she said calmly, 'you need to sit down.'

Her tone startled me a little.

'Your dad's name is Stewart. He left me when I was pregnant with you and, years later, got together with someone else we know.'

'Who?' I asked, puzzled.

'Mary. Your godmother.'

My mouth fell open.

'They've been divorced for years now, but yeah, she was married to your dad.'

This explained why Mary had been so cryptic with me and Nat and why her name seemed to be at the centre of the story coming out. There were no hard feelings between Mum and Mary; they had been friends forever. Mary sent me and Nat a birthday card with a fiver in it every year right up until we turned 21 and she had the most beautiful crochet blankets made for me when I had Josh and Jack. She had met Stewart a long time after he did a runner on Mum. It was all just a big messy coincidence with me in the middle.

I went back to Mary to tell her I knew, with Natalie by my side again for moral support.

'I'm sorry, Rachel,' she said. 'It just wasn't my place to tell you.'

'It's OK,' I said. 'It's all out in the open now, eh.'

'Do you know I had a couple of kids with him?'

'No.'

'Stewart and Sandra are his. They're your half-brother and sister.'

As if it had been rehearsed, the door opened and little Stewart came in from school. He was mid-teens and, like most boys his age, so filthy from the day he looked like he'd been rolling around in the road. I'd met Mary's kids before, but now I was looking at them in a whole new light. *My God, we look so alike!* I thought. *He's even got my dimples!*

'Do you want me to ring him?' Mary asked.

'Sorry?' I said, tearing my eyes away from little Stewart.

'Your dad. I can ring him if you like.'

'Yes!' Natalie said, before I could chicken out.

Mary picked up the phone and dialled.

'All right, Stew?' she said. 'Are you sat down? There's someone here who wants to meet you. It's Rachel … She knows you're her father.'

Big Stewart had been out weeding his garden. He said he needed ten minutes to freshen up then would be straight round. I sat waiting, my tummy churning away. *Did I really want to meet him? What if he was an arsehole?*

Before long there was a knock at the door and Mary got up to let him in. A man with my nose and forehead walked in and smiled.

'There she is,' I said, pointing to Natalie.

He laughed. 'I think I know who's mine.'

The man I met that day was very warm and welcoming. He was a laugh a minute – I could see why Mum and Mary had liked him – and I was quite surprised to pick up on the similarities in our characters. We agreed that he could take me out for Sunday lunch and I took the opportunity to quiz him some more.

'So why didn't you ever bother with us?' I asked.

'I just didn't want to upset the apple cart. Your mum was with Ray and, well, I was young and stupid.'

The whole thing could have been an epic *Jeremy Kyle* moment, but everyone involved just kind of took it on the chin. Mum understandably preferred to keep her distance from the situation, but Nat got on really well with the new additions to my family. Stewart and I just kind of slipped into each other's life for a while. There was never any pressure for him to be a dad because Colin had done an absolutely superb job of filling the role of stepfather and grandfather. It was just nice to have another portion of family in my life.

Darren was happy that I had finally got to the bottom of the family secret so I had no problem telling him when big Stewart invited me to the pub for a drink.

'Where you meeting him?' Darren asked.

'Oh, just the Prince of Wales,' I said. 'He's in there with a few of his mates.'

'You're not going there,' he said. 'It's too rough. It'll be full of dodgy bastards.'

I didn't know any better so I rang Stewart back and cancelled.

Chapter Ten

To my beautiful Valentine Rachel Girl,
Life is hard, love hurts and love makes you strong
Rachel the longer the years go by I realise you were and will always
be my one true Valentine
Your love makes me feel so good inside
Your Valentine,
Darren
I love ya

I never told a soul what Darren was really like at home. I minimised the violence in my head as a way of surviving, but knew that if my family and friends knew the truth they would be horrified. I didn't want to dump any of this at their door. I never wanted anyone else to be in the firing line and I didn't see what any of them could do about him anyway.

The truth was everybody had their suspicions. They all knew that Darren was the town troublemaker. They all picked up on the subtle changes in my behaviour, like never changing my hairstyle or going out and having fun the way I used to. I thought I was keeping a lid on things, rattling off water-tight excuses for the odd bruise on my arm. Darren hadn't broken me. I was still the same tough cookie I'd always been. I thought I could handle him and as much as everyone around me had their concerns, I think they probably believed I could too.

Mum always seemed to be asking when I was going to go out with the girls.

'I don't want to go out,' I'd say, with a shrug. 'I'm not interested.'

'Why not?' she'd ask. 'You know I'll babysit.'

I would have loved to call some girlfriends and arrange a night out to blow off some steam, but I couldn't face the hassle I'd get for it. Darren always had something negative to say about my friends – he thought Jayne was far too wild, for example – and in hindsight it was easier to distance myself from people than it was to keep seeing them.

I must have been feeling isolated because I would find myself organising get-togethers with Darren's family. He always resisted, of course.

'I don't know why you're fucking bothering,' he'd say. 'They're all fucking slags.'

But if we were going for a meal with his sisters at least I was getting out of the house. If it wasn't for them I would barely see anyone. No one ever came round to the house – not even Mum. Darren was not someone the people in my life wanted to be around.

With my thirtieth birthday coming up, Mum changed tack and told me about a coach trip to Paris she'd seen offered in one of the newspapers.

'You and Darren have never been away together just you two,' she said. 'You should go. Have some fun. Me and Colin will have the boys.'

I agreed. Things had been so stressful lately maybe a break was just what we needed. It would certainly be easier than telling Darren I was going on a night out with the girls.

I asked Mum if she would mind booking it for us. It was an absolute steal at £99 per person for travel and accommodation. Mum paid for my ticket as my birthday present and Darren gave her the money to cover his. This was a dream come true for him – all he had to do was turn up and have me to himself for a weekend.

It was one of those holidays where the coach takes you to your hotel to check in, then whisks you off sightseeing for the day. We walked hand in hand staring up at the Eiffel Tower and marvelled at the stunning Palace of Versailles, where we drank hot chocolate in the visitors' cafe. The weather was cold, but stayed dry. Holidays were usually so stressful, but for some reason, this one felt easy – the way I imagined holidays were supposed to feel. I'm not sure if Darren went so far as buying me a thirtieth birthday gift, but there would have definitely been a card telling me I was the most perfect girl on the planet. Mum was right: Paris had been exactly what we needed. I came back hopeful that maybe we were coming out of the horrible rut we'd been in.

Back home I was sitting in bed doing my make-up while Darren had a shower. When he'd finished he came into the bedroom with a towel wrapped around his waist.

'There's stuff coming out of my old boy,' he said, gesturing to his privates.

'What do you mean?' I said.

'There's stuff coming out of it.'

'That's not right.'

'I bet it's that soap I've been using,' he said. He did still get sensitive skin from time to time.

'You should go to the doctors just in case,' I said. 'It might be an infection.'

'Yeah, I will. I'm going to the GUM clinic with a friend. He thinks he's got something and wants to get checked. I might as well see someone while I'm there.'

The friend was someone who lived in Cardiff and at the time I thought nothing of them going off on this oddly prearranged trip to the clinic together. Darren phoned me afterwards to say he'd got an infection. He said it was nothing to worry about – we would simply need to take a short course of medication to make sure we were both treated. It never entered my head to question what it was or where the infection might have come from. I just got on the phone to my doctor, told them what Darren had been advised and organised a prescription.

I was still working at Bonkerz but the idea of branching out on my own as a mobile hairdresser was really starting to appeal to me. There had been some bickering among the staff at the salon and the atmosphere wasn't great. One day I went out the back to put some towels on the line to dry and, when I came back in, two of the girls were having a cat fight. I tried to separate them but they carried on going at it like I was invisible. I grabbed hold of them by the hair and, using my foot to open the back door, shoved them outside to carry on. They made so much noise somebody called the police!

Frances left the business shortly after that and I took it as my cue to move on. Without her around, I didn't have any guilt about taking a couple of clients with me. I told a few of my regulars I was going solo and they said they were happy to keep using me. With my salon clients and all the family and friends who wanted me to do their hair from home I had a ready-made mobile hairdressing business.

To outsiders I was doing well for myself, but behind closed doors the magic of Paris had long worn off. I was back to feeling like a single mum, going to parents' evening on my own. Darren never spent time with the boys or took them anywhere. He came to one nativity play and I could feel him next to me hating every minute of it.

'It's like being in a stinking leisure centre being around all these kids,' he scoffed.

All Darren cared about was going to the gym, having enough money for steroids and what crime documentary he was going to watch next.

My coping strategy was to keep busy and avoid him as much as I could, but that wasn't possible 100 per cent of the time. When we ended up in the house together he would nearly always start. He would pace about behind me, grinding his teeth and breathing heavily. He would call me a lazy bitch or a slag. If I turned my back on him I would get a jab to the back of the head. If I stood up to him he would spit in my face. The spitting was just the lowest of the low for me. I can't think of many things more degrading than that. The tear-stained apologies would come as regular as clockwork, but the behaviour went on and on.

Darren was still driving for the agency and had been getting a lot of work for Asda. This meant that, when a full-time job came up there, he was already in line for the position. I never thought I'd see the day that Darren would work for a supermarket chain, but he went for it and got the job. I think it helped that he had made a good friend there. Brian was a lovely guy in his sixties. He had worked for Asda for years, and I think he understood the type of man Darren was and wanted to take him under his wing.

This worked out well for me as I got on like a house of fire with Brian's wife, Ann. We met at a sixtieth birthday party for one of Brian and Darren's work colleagues, and over drinks we chatted about how nice it would be to meet again for dinner, just the four of us. I went out of my way to make sure it happened. With my social life hanging by a thread, I was delighted to have another couple to hang out with and kind of clung on to their friendship. They were older and wiser, and I think Ann suspected I was a bit of a caged bird. The four of us would go out for a curry or we'd go to theirs and Ann would cook. They were really good company and because Darren didn't mind driving I could enjoy a drink.

Darren thought the world of Brian, which was encouraging because he didn't like anyone. Unfortunately, he was very unpleasant about Ann. He would say things like, 'She's got a head like a fucking horse that one.' He thought she was a bighead because she had thoughts and opinions. She spoke her mind and was treated as Brian's equal, which Darren could never get his head around.

Despite this, we grew so close to Brian and Ann that in 2003 we had a long weekend in Prague together. With Jack and Josh enjoying some precious Mum and Colin time, we caught a flight from Bristol airport, stayed in a lovely hotel and filled our time pottering about, eating, drinking, sightseeing and shopping.

Darren was the type of man who couldn't walk past a beggar without giving them money. I was the same, but not when I was on holiday and on a tight budget. So when we passed a woman asking for money in Prague's Old Town Square, I instinctively went for the change in my purse. This angered Darren.

'I want a fucking note,' he snapped, grabbing my purse and taking out all the Czech banknotes.

'What are you doing,' I said in an angry whisper, 'that's all our money!'

'Don't fucking tell me I can't spend my money!' he boomed.

I felt so embarrassed that he was speaking to me like this in front of Brian and Ann.

Darren gave the beggar some cash then marched back up to me to carry on having a go. I stared up at the famous astronomical clock, trying to blank him while he bent down right in my face trying to get a reaction. When I walked away he started on Brian and Ann.

'What the fuck's she playing at not giving me the money?' he asked.

They didn't respond because they knew Darren was not a man you could argue with, but their silence spoke volumes. They weren't giving Darren the backup he was expecting, which made it clear to him they didn't agree with how he'd just behaved.

An hour later he was really sorry and trying to brush it all under the carpet.

'Come on, Rach. Just forget it,' he said.

Ann and I exchanged a look. Inside I was screaming: *He's such a bastard!* And I think she was communicating her sympathy and support. I turned my head away from Darren. He had shown me up and belittled me in front of people I really cared about. But once I'd cooled off I put my brave face on. I couldn't bear the awkwardness and was extra nice to Darren in front of Brian and Ann so he had no choice but to reciprocate.

Before the four of us flew home from Prague we went out on one last shopping trip. We were headed up an escalator in a shopping centre when Darren saw something reflected in the mirrored panels to our side.

'What's that down there?' he said, spinning round. We got to the top of the escalator and had to come straight back down again. Darren had seen a shop selling weapons and he couldn't get in there fast enough.

'I wanna see what they got here.'

It wasn't my scene so I let him have a look round. I couldn't help but be a bit taken aback when he decided to buy a stun gun and some CS gas.

'Why you want those for, Da?' I asked.

'Just in case, love.'

'Can you take it on the plane though?'

'We'll have to see, won't we?'

I can't remember how much these things cost but I know I had to hand over my credit card. Darren didn't care that it was the end of the holiday and we'd spent all our money – he wanted to buy what he wanted to buy.

When it was time to catch the plane home all I could think about was what was in Darren's suitcase. I could tell Brian and Ann were on edge too, and when we landed at Bristol airport the three of us walked off ahead of Darren, distancing ourselves from the potential drama. By some miracle, he never got stopped and was able to bring the items home. He put them with his hunting knives in the drawer on his side of our divan bed.

After that trip, whenever we talked about other places we could visit for holidays or city breaks, Darren would always want to find out if you could buy weapons out there. We looked at Poland and I invited Darren's father and his new wife Carol because I knew she had always wanted to go. I thought it would be good for us all to spend some time together but the only reason Darren agreed to go was so he could go to the weapons stores. Every holiday was an excuse to buy something – flick knives, pepper spray – anything he couldn't get his hands on over here. I let him get on with it. If he was obsessing over his hobbies at least he was leaving me alone.

Despite having such a good relationship with Brian, Darren never quite took to his job working for Asda. He was the type of man who resisted authority. They sent him here, there and everywhere and, although that was probably just what was expected of someone in his role, he felt they were taking the piss out of him. After a while he said he was going to make working there 'worth his while'. And I soon found out what he meant.

Darren started stealing cigarettes from his load so he could sell them on for a profit. It started with small amounts but, as he got more confident, quickly became larger and larger quantities. Once he got a handle on the system, he got other drivers involved too – taking cigarettes from their trailers and giving them half the proceeds once he sold them on. This went on for months. I was a bag of nerves because I knew it would catch up with us one day.

Darren used the extra money he made to pay for us to have a conservatory built on the back of the house and once that was finished he set his sights higher.

'I want to set up a business,' he said.

'What kind of business?' I asked.

'A catering van.'

I agreed it could be a nice little earner, but knew full well Darren would not be able to do it alone. He did not have the patience needed to be his own boss or deal with customers. Plus, the only thing he'd ever cooked was beans on toast for me when I was ill. But he found a second-hand van and through a friend we managed to rent a site for it at our local docks. My sister Nat agreed to help. Darren didn't want me serving under any circumstances as almost all the customers were going to be men, so we agreed that I would prepare and deliver the stock for the day and Nat would be front of house. All Darren had to do was collect the van from the yard each morning and position it down at the docks, ready for us to open up.

We took advantage of the passing trade, selling cooked breakfasts, fresh rolls, salad boxes and jacket potatoes. Every day we had a special, which would be something like a chili or curry that I would make the night before. I spent every Sunday scrubbing the van to make sure it was spotless again for Monday. In summer, when business was good and it was too hot for Darren's dogs to be out hunting, he would help me clean. He made it clear that if the van wasn't up to scratch we wouldn't be allowed to open and I didn't want that on my head.

This would have been a great business in the hands of the right person, but Darren wasn't the right person. Nat and I were perfectly capable of looking after things, but instead of leaving us to it, Darren was constantly sticking his oar in and losing his temper over the slightest thing. To get to the trailer we had to drive over a railway crossing. One morning when I was delivering the bread rolls, a train went past and I had to wait. Darren was in the docks for work and had stopped by to check on things. When I arrived with the rolls, he lost it because I was three minutes late. He smacked the tray up in the air, sending the rolls flying, then I was half strangled round the back of the van. One of the dock workers saw the whole thing and told Nat.

'That man's an animal,' he said. 'I'm never eating here again.'

Nat was so upset I sent her home and we had no choice but to close for the day. That afternoon I got a huge bouquet of flowers. As I shoved them half-heartedly in some water, I realised that I only ever got flowers when Darren was feeling guilty for hurting me.

Every other day me and Darren would argue; about the van and over fights he had gotten into when he was working on the door. I had been happy for him to carry on doing the work, simply to guarantee myself some peace on Friday and Saturday nights. But even his job as a bouncer was getting out of control. Darren had become known as The Drag Net, on account of his ability to scoop groups of people up and get them outside. This was part of his job, I guess, but unfortunately, if any of these people offended

Darren he would respond with his fists. I got wind that men were being beaten up and chucked down flights of stairs. There were reports of people being knocked clean out. The police were always being called, but by the time they arrived Darren would have vanished. I wondered if the cameras he installed at the house were to give him a heads up if the police were outside, but he rarely had any comebacks because people were so frightened of him. You would get the odd person try to push it further, but the complaint would always be dropped. Someone always knew someone.

Darren developed a real hatred for the police. Even though he was the one doing things he shouldn't have been, he felt they were out to get him.

'These fucking police,' he'd say, 'they're nothing but a bunch of jumped-up twats. They got bullied in school and now they think they can bully everyone else.'

On one occasion, one of the licensees who employed Darren was summoned to see the Police Chief Constable who told him: 'If I hear one more complaint about Darren Williams I will personally lift him myself.'

There were so many incidents that I lost track. Unsurprisingly, the owners of the pub and club had no choice but to ask Darren to leave, saying he was 'too much of a liability'. To add further complications, a new law was being introduced that required all doormen to pass a recognised training course. If you had a clean police record and passed the course, you got a badge that deemed you officially trained door staff. This put a stop to any hopes Darren had of extending his career on the door. He couldn't even apply for the course because he had a criminal conviction from before he met me, for head-butting a paramedic who had been trying to help him after an overdose.

On the one hand, I felt relieved this part of Darren's life had come to an end. But on the other, my peaceful weekends were now coming to an end too.

Chapter Eleven

To My Darling Rachel
11 years together
I can't imagine all these years with anybody else
U are the most prettyest girl in the world
I love you so much I really do

It was only £100 a week, but now he had lost his cash in hand from working as a doorman, Darren got greedier and greedier with his cigarette scam. I begged him to stop.

'It will catch up with us,' I warned him. 'It's only a matter of time.'

He got word that a security guard at Asda was on to him, but he was so cocky about it by this point that nothing was going to stop him. Darren got a huge kick out of not just the stealing, but the cat-and-mouse game that was going on between him and the security guard – and him and the police. He thought he was always one step ahead.

The day Darren's luck ran out, he was on a delivery in Didcot, near Oxford. He pulled his truck over into a lay-by and the police who had been following him took their opportunity to pounce. They found cases of cigarettes that Darren had hidden in the bushes. His little earner was over.

The first whiff of trouble I got was when I tried Darren's mobile and got no answer. When the phone rang, I thought he was just returning my call but he was calling from the police station to break the news that he'd been busted.

'Rach, best get the solicitor,' he said. 'I'm really fucked this time.'

My heart sank. I knew, if Darren was fucked, I would soon be getting the brunt of his emotions.

'You know that thing in the shed,' he said cryptically, 'the thing of Dylan's, just make sure it's moved.'

Darren had a garden gun down there – a small pistol used to shoot vermin which was classed as an illegal weapon. My heart was pounding. *Shit!* I thought. I put the phone down and was about to turn on my heels and go straight to the shed when I heard a knock at the door. It was the police.

'Are you the partner of Mr Darren Williams?'

'Yes.'

'He's been arrested on suspicion of theft. We have a warrant to search your property.'

I let them in.

'We'd like to go up in the attic if that's OK.'

'Yeah, course,' I said. 'I'll get you the step ladders.'

I paced about nervously as they began their search. There was no way I could get to the gun now. *Darren's gonna fucking kill me,* I thought. When one of the officers went out to the shed, I held my breath waiting for a sign they'd found the gun, but he came out empty-handed. I went upstairs to find another officer looking through our bedroom. I had nothing to hide in here and my mind was still fixated on the gun in the shed, but as he was rummaging through my personal things I felt I should stay and supervise. He bent down to look under the bed and knocked his knee on the handle of the divan drawer which had been hidden by the trim of the Valance sheet. If he hadn't done that he wouldn't have known the drawers were there. He lifted the sheet on Darren's side, pulled open the drawer and, after a few moments of silence, shouted to his colleagues downstairs: 'You'd better get the sergeant.'

They had come to the house looking for cigarettes or evidence of the theft and stumbled upon Darren's stash of weapons. The drawer contained a pistol, a stun gun, a catapult gun, the CS gas, pepper spray, flick knives, telescopic truncheons and various hunting knives – more items than I care to remember. It sounds alarming now, but I knew what he collected and had long since detached myself from it. Anything Darren did – the gym, the dogs, the crime books and documentaries – was of no interest to me. However, these weapons *were* of great interest to the police. They packed them all carefully into evidence bags and took them off to the station. Darren was in even deeper shit than we thought.

Darren was kept in Oxford overnight then transferred back to Newport the following day where he was questioned at our local police station about the weapons. He claimed he was just a collector and insisted he had no intention of ever using them, but they had enough evidence to charge him with possession. He arrived home on bail in a foul mood.

'How the fuck did they find the weapons?' he barked angrily.

'One of them found the drawer,' I said. 'I'm sorry, Da, they were knocking the door as soon as I got off the phone to you. I didn't have time to think.'

We met with Gareth, a solicitor who worked with my mum. He warned us that Darren could be facing a prison sentence, and a harsh one at that. New laws on firearms were just being introduced giving the courts more power to impose tougher sentences. Darren could be looking at five years. The timing couldn't have been worse.

Darren insisted I go to court to support him so I spent the short hearing sat in the gallery of Cardiff Crown Court with his father. It was a reasonably cut-and-dried case – there was no evidence Darren had used any of the illegal weapons, but he *had* been caught red-handed with them in the house. The judge found him guilty of possession; he was definitely facing prison.

I sat looking at the judge awaiting our fate and saw one of the lenses fall out of her glasses. It landed on her desk with such a clunk I had to try really hard not to laugh. Darren's father (who had no such restraint) let out a snigger. He got an evil look from his son that said, 'Don't you fucking dare.'

Darren was sentenced to four months in prison and marched down to the cells there and then. My very first thought was how peaceful the house was going to be without him. Outside the court, our solicitor Gareth was deep in conversation with a colleague. Darren's sentence had been lighter than we'd expected and they wondered if the judge had made a mistake. The guy even suggested going back into the court.

'You'll do no such thing,' Gareth replied. 'Darren's been sentenced, let's leave it be.'

I went home and told the boys that Darren would not be coming home for a while, although I couldn't help but wonder if they would even miss him. Josh was 14 now and couldn't really care less. Jack took it harder, but then it *was* his dad and he was still only 10. He was still very close to me, just like he was as a baby. If Darren got up early, Jack would always come and get into bed with me for a cuddle. Darren would joke that the umbilical cord had never been cut and I would wonder if there was some jealousy there. I saw Jack's soft side, but he was also a strong character that liked to stick up for the underdog. Even if it was just Mum having a go at Colin for not getting the washing in, Jack would be the one jumping to Colin's defence.

'Can I come visit Dad in prison?' Jack asked.

I told him if that was what he wanted, then that was what we would do.

Darren sent us a visiting order as soon as he could with strict instructions to bring plenty of change for the vending machines. The prison food was terrible so he would want to fill up on chocolate and sweets. The day of the visit there was a lot of waiting around and more than a few unsavoury characters visiting other inmates. Luckily, Jack seemed to find the whole thing a bit of an adventure. When we finally got to Darren, he was sat with his chest all puffed up like he was trying to make a point.

'How are you coping?' I asked.

'They're all a bunch of pussies in here,' he sneered between bites of a Snickers bar.

I knew Darren would have no trouble looking after himself in prison. He was so big that nobody was going to mess with him.

With Darren behind bars it fell on my shoulders to keep the catering van going. Every day I had to pick it up from the yard where we kept it locked up and tow it to and from the docks. I'd had one brief towing lesson from Darren before his court case and he'd spat on me because I didn't get it right. It wasn't easy, but I soon mastered it. I think on some level I wanted to prove to him that I could do it.

As well as the catering van, I was booked up to my eyeballs with hairdressing work. It was manic, but without Darren around everything felt so much easier. I even managed to squeeze in sharing a bottle of wine on a Friday night with my friend Claire, a mum I'd grown close to after meeting her at the school gates.

The weeks flew by and, before I knew it, I was getting a call from Gareth to say Darren was being released. As long as he agreed to wear a tag and adhere to a curfew, he could come home. He had served just seven weeks of his sentence; I wished it had been more.

One of the first things Darren did when he got home was pick up his hunting knives from the police station. The police had destroyed the gun, but because Darren had argued the knives were collector's items and not for use, legally they had to give them back. Darren took great pleasure in going to the station and asking for them; anything to get one up on the police.

Meanwhile, the cigarette case rumbled on and on. It was much more complex in terms of pulling together evidence and Darren was tetchy. He had got off lightly with the weapons charge and coped well with a reasonably short stint inside. But the novelty of being home was short-lived with another prison stretch hanging over him.

The police had the cigarettes that Darren had stashed in the bushes, but he was adamant they would not be able to link him to them as he had worn gloves whenever he handled the bags. The case dragged on for months until we received a letter from Gareth saying Darren's print had been found on a tube of superglue, a tube that had been in the same bag as a bundle of stolen cigarettes. The jig was up.

Chapter Twelve

To My Darling Rachel
(soon to be my wife)
I could never spend a Christmas with another
You are the one
The only one for me
Til the end my lover
Your Dazo
xxxx

On 22 July 2005, Darren was back in court to face the music. He was found guilty and sentenced to another nine months inside. To make matters more complicated, because he had been caught on one of his delivery runs down in Oxford, that is where the trial was held and that was where he went to prison. It was nearly a two-hour drive away and he hated it.

I was under strict instructions to get him moved closer to home as soon as possible and he would phone me at every opportunity to see what I was doing about it.

I contacted our local MP and played on Darren's mental-health situation, explaining he suffered with anxiety and depression and that prison officers were not giving him his medication at regular times. This wasn't a complete lie – they weren't great at dishing out the meds and it did have an effect on his well-being – but I certainly didn't care as much as I made out. I couldn't help but feel free with Darren out of the house again. I caused such a fuss with the authorities that I'm sure they agreed to move Darren just to get me off their case – which in turn got Darren off mine.

Without him around, me and Nat were able to make easy work of managing the van, bringing in around four to five hundred pounds a week. I think Darren half expected me to crumble. But after a few visits he second he realise that I wasn't crying into my pillow every night; I was coping just fine without him – better even.

While he was waiting for his transfer back to Wales, Darren's attitude towards me changed. He suddenly became softer and more appreciative of me. He sent letter after letter professing his love, saying how painful it was being apart and how he was never going to let it happen again. When I visited he was affectionate and we were able to share a laugh and a joke for the first time in what felt like years. The space prison gave us, and without his temper rearing its ugly head, I was able to see a side to Darren that I'd started to forget existed. I wondered if prison would be the making of him and maybe even our relationship. Still, I hadn't been expecting it when I got the call.

'Rach, I think we should get married.'

It was the second marriage proposal of my life and still no man down on one knee. I couldn't help but laugh. The first was from a hospital bed and the second from prison. He didn't even say 'Will you marry me?' And just like the first time, I was being proposed to by a man at a difficult time in his life and didn't feel able to say no. I knew that if I didn't give Darren the answer he wanted he would be crushed, probably even suicidal. We had been together for 12 years now and I knew one thing for sure: marrying Darren would be a whole lot easier than leaving him.

Dear Darling Rachel,

Rach, this is a fucking shithole. I need to get transferred to Wales hopefully ASAP but the main reason because you can't get up here every week. No good for my fucking head.

My love please be strong for me and don't do anything to make me worry (dos and don'ts haha) I miss you all over again, it fucking hurts. I love you so much and when we're apart it makes me realise how much more this will be the last time.

Rach, I was serious about getting married, really, no jokes or because I feel down (cause I fucking do) it's just you've proved your love for me time and time again, please don't think I don't feel the same because you'd be very wrong. So start making arrangements for us to get married please. We were meant to be together my love.

Send my love to Jack and Josh.

Can't write no more, trying to stay strong.

See you Sunday bye for now

All my love

Your Dazo

Xxxx

PS. Dreams can come true!

Darren told me to start organising the wedding using cash he had hidden in our downstairs toilet. There was a secret compartment beneath the sink that he'd put in when we decorated. When I looked my mouth fell open. There must have been hundreds, all in rolled-up five-pound notes.

'Use whatever cash is in there,' he said.

I told the boys that we were going to be getting married. If Josh thought it was a bad idea he didn't let it show. Jack seemed more excited, but only because he liked the idea of the big party.

I went into autopilot, booking a country club for that December and finding a dress. I didn't put a huge amount of time and thought into things, I just chose the cheapest wedding breakfast and bought the first dress I didn't hate. I didn't realise it at the time, but I was not a woman looking forward to getting married. Whenever I saw Darren and updated him on everything, he always seemed really pleased with me. Although he detested being in prison again, his positivity towards me was encouraging. He had always said he would never get married because his parents' marriage was such a disaster and yet here he was, prepared to make that commitment.

Darren was released from prison on 5 December 2005 and we tied the knot right after Christmas on 29 December. The morning of the wedding I got ready at the house with Josh and Jack. My dress was a world away from the blancmange I'd worn when I married Ian. It was a bustier design and very straight, something classy and not too fussy – something I knew Darren would like.

Brian had offered to drive me to the club in his lovely old Jaguar, so when the door went I assumed it would be him.

'Rachel?'

There was a man in a suit stood on my doorstep and it wasn't Brian.

'Yes?'

I could see a cream-coloured vintage wedding car parked up on the street behind him.

'I've come to take you to your wedding. Darren arranged it.'

My first thought was, *How has he paid for this?*

The car took me and the boys to the venue and, although it was very beautiful, it was so old it had gaps everywhere. When we had to travel a short distance along the motorway the three of us were absolutely freezing.

I arrived at the venue bang on time (as if I would have dared be late), took a deep breath and set off down the aisle. There was no one there to give me away this time. Now I had a stepfather, an adoptive father and a biological father, I felt that asking any one of them would be unkind to the others. The significance of it years later, however, is quite astonishing: walking to my fate alone, looking strong but secretly feeling trapped.

As I walked towards Darren, he turned his head and smiled. I felt nothing, other than a twinge of relief that he looked pleased.

'Did you like your car?' he whispered.

'How did you pay for it?' I asked.

'I borrowed the cash off Mum. I wanted to surprise you. It's my wedding gift.'

I remember feeling liked I'd proved myself by waiting for Darren, by planning the wedding and keeping the catering business afloat. And yet I never felt like he was in awe of me as I stood there in my ivory dress. It almost felt like he was the star and I should be grateful he was marrying me. The whole day was for Darren, really, anything to keep him happy and spare myself his tantrums. Apart from swearing at someone who dared ask him where the registrar was, he was in a reasonably good mood the whole day. And yet when I think back to how many guests turned up, there weren't that many. Most of them were family or friends of mine. Darren didn't have many friends and the ones he did have were scared of him. It wasn't the wedding party of the century, put it that way. I don't think anyone who knew me felt great about me marrying this man. I guess they thought I must know what I was doing.

Some months later I heard that, during the reception, my friend Jayne said to my mother, 'Congratulations, Avril, you've got the son-in-law from hell.'

Chapter Thirteen

To my darling wife, my Rachel girl
My wife with the face of an angel
Merry Merry Christmas my love
(Our first Chrimbo as man and wife)
Love and kisses my star
All my love now and forever
Your mad husband
Darren
xxxx

A good wedding can be so wonderful that it feels like someone waving a magic wand over your life. But, as most newlyweds will tell you, once it's all over the fairy dust wears off very quickly. For me and Darren, the injection of sparkle and hope was even more fleeting. I'm not even sure I felt any magic at all.

The New Year came and went and life just snapped back to the same old keep-busy-and-get-by routine. I ran my mobile hairdressing business during the day and prepared food for the catering van in the evenings. I was worried Darren's conviction would stop him getting a job, but thankfully he was still able to get some full-time driving work through the agency. I was relieved – not just because it meant we had more money coming in, but because he would be occupied. The more he worked and went to the gym, and the more he buried his head in books about Charles Bronson, the less I had to deal with him.

My life had become about avoiding Darren at all costs. Our physical relationship had been very loving and affectionate in the beginning, but now he was 23 stone I couldn't bear him on top of me, out of breath and sweating everywhere. If I could be in bed asleep before him, I would make sure I was. Sometimes I would pretend to be asleep so he wouldn't bother me. Every ten days or so I would endure sex – this was to satisfy him on my own terms and so he wouldn't realise I was avoiding it the rest of the time. I was trapped in the bare bones of a relationship. He'd given me two years of heaven and ten years of hell and it had taken its toll.

We agreed to wrap up the catering business about a year after Darren came out of prison. With us both in steady work we decided we could live without the money and the stress, and, as luck would have it, we were able to sell it straight back to the guy we bought it from, no questions asked.

Darren was 40 now. I don't know if he was easing off on the steroids but he seemed to be mellowing a little – although for someone like Darren that wasn't saying much. The incidents of violence were happening slightly less often, but the threat of it was still very much in the air. I was on eggshells constantly because there was always a chance of Darren throwing something or grabbing me by the hair. Even when he was out I couldn't get away from him. He would ring me to mouth off about the slightest thing that was happening during his day. I could get a phone call at any time and woe betide me if I ignored it. I was like his mother, counsellor, doctor and punch bag all rolled into one.

We still argued a lot. The most frustrating fights we had were the ones that started from nothing. Living with two hungry boys and a man Darren's size was like living with termites. To give you an example of how bad it was, I started hiding chocolate in the tumble dryer to make it last all week. I was a big fan of Marmite crisps and one day I hid the last packet on a shelf behind some dishes so no one else would have them. But when I went to get them, they were gone. Darren was in the living room with Melvin, a mate from the gym.

'What's happened to my crisps?' I asked.

'I ate 'em,' he said.

'No, you haven't,' I said, thinking he was joking.

'I have. They're there to be eaten.'

'I can't believe you, Darren,' I said, heading back into the kitchen. 'I was looking forward to them.'

And just like that, he went from zero to a hundred.

'Are you really going to go on about a fucking packet of crisps?' he boomed.

He was on his feet now, riled up and red in the face. He came over to the kitchen, literally frothing at the mouth.

Thankfully, Melvin cut in. 'Darren,' he shouted. 'Calm the fuck down!'

If Melvin hadn't been there things could have been a lot worse, but I still got an apple chucked at the back of my head – all because the greedy bastard ate *my* crisps! It was ridiculous.

Darren still wrote cards professing his love for me but the messages seemed to be taking a darker turn. He would say that we were together in a previous life and that we would always be together in this life and the next. No one ever saw the cards.

They would be on the side for a couple of days then I would store them away.

By this time, every time we argued I threatened to leave. Although I still spared them the worst, I would rant to my sister and friend Claire that I was done, that the relationship was over and I wanted nothing more to do with Darren. I would say it to the boys – who would half-listen sympathetically then get back to their computer games assuming I probably wouldn't go through with it. I even said it to Darren himself. If the bust-up had been bad Darren would cry and say he wanted to kill himself. Other times he would just laugh and say: 'There's only one way out for you, Rachel, and that's in a wooden box.' I was never sure if he was joking or not. He said the same thing to some neighbours of ours too. When they didn't see me for a few days and saw Darren dragging the wheelie bin outside they were worried I was in it. I knew I wanted out, but I still didn't know how I was going to pull it off.

Darren hadn't worked on the door for over a year, but still couldn't seem to stay on the right side of trouble. I was putting a jacket potato in the microwave when he walked through the door with a face on.

'That's CID outside,' he said, gesturing to the window.

I looked out and sure enough there were two men sat across the street in an unmarked car.

'How do you know?' I asked.

'I just do,' he said. 'I can tell.'

Darren plonked himself down on the sofa. I went back to the kitchen, turned the microwave on, then heard a knock at the door. I paused to see if Darren was going to get up off his arse and answer it. When I heard no movement, I went to the hall to open the door.

'Is Mr Williams there?'

It was the two men from the car. I stood back so they could see through to Darren in the living room.

'Can we come in?' they asked, about to step inside.

'No, you fucking can't,' Darren shouted from the sofa, stopping them in their tracks.

'We just need to speak to you about—'

'I'm having my fucking dinner!' he snapped angrily. Darren jumped to his feet, ready to shut the door in their faces. I stood back to let him do it, only for one of the coppers to stick his foot in the way. Darren was fuming.

'Get your fucking foot out of my door or I'll bury you.'

The copper – clearly bricking it – did as he was told and took a step back. He might have been a policeman but he was no match for a man of Darren's size.

'Can we speak to you after your tea?'

'I'll give you a nod,' Darren said, slamming the door.

The men went back to their car and waited while Darren ate his jacket potato.

'You're going to have to go and ask them what it's about,' I said. 'What have you done?'

'Fuck all!' he said.

When he realised they weren't going to go away, Darren finally relented and invited them in. They explained that a local druggie was being questioned about a crime and had been using Darren's name as some kind of protection from other criminals.

They just wanted to know if Darren knew anything but he was clueless to the whole thing.

'Take me down the station with you,' Darren said, 'I'll get the truth out of him.'

He actually thought he was helping.

'Er, no, Mr Williams. Thanks, but we can't do that. Sorry to have disturbed you.'

I thought that was the end of it, but a couple of weeks later Darren sent me to a supermarket car park to pick something up. He wouldn't say what. When I arrived, a man came over to my car and handed me a carrier bag through my window. There was £500 cash in there – a payment from the druggie for using Darren's name. I drove home and gave Darren the money, seething internally that I had been dragged into his dodgy dealings again.

My patience was wearing thin and I started to wonder if my opinion of Darren could ever be repaired. Everything he said and did seemed tainted now. Even his hunting – which had always seemed like a reasonably healthy hobby – was starting to feel sinister. One morning, I was putting some washing on the line when I heard a strange crying sound. I peered round to the yard where the kennels were and saw a cat in a wire cage. It was pacing and whining, looking really distressed. Darren was still in bed when I went back inside to ask him why there was a cat in a cage in our garden.

'None of your fucking business,' he snapped, rolling over and going back to sleep.

When I finally heard him get up and go out the back, I peered out of a window to watch what he did. He kept a radio by the kennels, which he would leave on to help keep the dogs quiet. To my horror, he turned the radio to full blast, grabbed the cat by the scruff of its neck and threw it to the dogs. They ripped the poor thing apart while the radio drowned out the noise. When I asked him about it later Darren said it was to 'bring the dogs on', to give them a taste of blood ready for hunting, like it was the most normal thing in the world.

If his dogs didn't work well he just got rid of them. For years I thought he was giving them away to a good home but he wasn't – he would kill them. When a female dog killed one of her pups, Darren was so furious that he smashed her head in with a shovel. I was so distressed I just ran inside and turned the TV up. When the dog was dead he stuffed her in a black bag and threw her in the river. How could you not be affected by that? But if I said anything, Darren would just shrug it off and say; 'Don't be a sissy.'

Up until now all the dogs we had were Darren's dogs. They lived outside and he would walk them or take them hunting. They were his hobby and, although Jack might feed them occasionally, they were never what me and the boys would call pets. But sometime in 2008 I was cutting my friend Tanya's hair when she asked if I knew anyone who wanted a puppy. Her son was about to become a dad so wanted to give his Staffordshire Bull Terrier to a good home. I knew the dog she meant – I remembered him biting my shoes once when I'd been cutting Tanya's hair. He was only about eight months old and very cute.

I'm such a soft touch with stuff like that that I rang Darren to ask if we could have him. I didn't worry that he might mistreat this one because he wasn't a hunting dog, he would be *our* dog. Darren said yes, so we moved him in and called him Scooby. He was the only dog allowed in the house because he was so daft and docile. He would come inside and lie on a blanket while we watched TV, and Jack loved to walk him round Brynglas Woods. We finally had a proper pet.

I took on a couple of cleaning jobs to fill my time between mobile hairdressing. One of them was for a doctor's surgery and I was given the keys so I could nip in and clean whenever suited me. I also saw a job advertised for a stylist at Carol Ann's hair salon on Malpas Road. It was only two days a week – Mondays and Tuesdays – so I applied for that too. Darren was OK about it because everyone knew it was the kind of salon that all the old dears liked to use. There was no way I'd be getting chatted up in there. I got the job, anything to keep busy and keep the money coming in. If we wanted money for extras like holidays then one of us had to.

Apart from work, the only respite I had away from Darren was time with my friend Claire. We still liked to share our bottle of wine on a Friday night when Darren was at the gym. I always held off talking about the violence, but if he was being a moody bastard I wouldn't hold back in slagging him off. It felt good to have someone to confide in, even if it was only a little bit. I'd spent so long feeling cut off from other women I really valued our friendship. We would have the odd girls' day out – shopping, lunch, that sort of thing. Darren approved of Claire because she was married and not too wild or opinionated, so I hung on to our time together for dear life.

We were about to set off in my car for one of our shopping trips when my phone rang. It was Nikki, a friend of mine. She was a police officer, which would have been a huge no-no for Darren had we not known her since she was 14. Her nanna was a neighbour we had grown very fond of over the years.

'Rach, Darren is wanted for questioning over an assault. Can he come down to the station? Otherwise they will come and get him.'

This type of phone call was not shocking or surprising to me. There was always someone making an allegation about Darren.

He was a few feet away from me, working under the bonnet of his Land Rover.

'Hang on,' I said to Nikki, 'I'll just pass the phone to him.'

I got out of my car and walked over to Darren.

'Darren, Nikki's on the phone. She needs to speak to you.'

He lifted his head and glared at me. He wasn't happy, but he took the call. I walked back to Claire and sat chatting with the window open, waiting for him to bring my phone back. After a few minutes, I looked up to see Darren walking over. I felt uneasy. He hated the police with a passion.

He chucked the phone at me and said, 'You ever fucking ring the police on me again, I will kill you.'

Before I could respond, Darren thrust his arm through the open window grabbed me by the hair and shoved my head backwards and forwards with such force that my head hit the rear-view mirror and broke it off. Claire was screaming. When Darren finally stormed off, I looked down and we were both covered in clumps of my hair. For Claire, this was a horrific thing to witness, but to me it was just Darren.

I started the car and sped off in a fury. *How dare he,* I thought. *How dare he ruin my one day out with Claire.* I was so mad that after a few minutes I found myself turning the car around and going back to the house to have it out with him. I marched upstairs to find him sat on the bed in tears.

'What the fuck do you think you're playing at?' I shouted.

'I'm so sorry, Rach,' he sobbed. 'I'm disgusting. I hate myself.'

'I can't believe you've just done that in front of Claire. I'm fuming.'

'I know, I'm sorry. I wish I was dead.'

'Pull yourself together,' I snapped. 'Get yourself washed and dressed and get down the station. Now!'

He rose to his feet and I left him to get sorted out. I knew Daniel was back and he would do exactly as he was told.

'Right,' I said to Claire as I got back in the car, 'let's go get a drink.'

I drove us to a pub where I let rip about how much I hated him.

'I'd love to just disappear,' I told her. 'To get away from him and live my life.'

Claire was sympathetic to my dilemma: where would I go? How would I uproot the boys? And if Darren was behaving like this when we were together how was he going to react if I left?

I started to fret about what kind of example Darren was setting for Josh and Jack. They didn't see everything but they had lived with him their whole lives. They knew he was nuts, there was no hiding what he was like. Darren never directed any of his anger onto them – that was all saved especially for me – but he was a terrible parent, really. He had no interest in enforcing even the most basic discipline. He would rather leave all that to me, then take the piss out of me for it. Now Jack was in his teens, Darren was more like one of the boys than a dad to them. Even Jack himself would say: 'It's like you're the kid and I'm the grown-up.'

Everyone called Jack 'Sparrow' because he loved the *Pirates of the Caribbean* films, but Darren also had a habit of referring to him as his 'one and only son'. I found this strange because I never felt like he treated Jack and Josh any differently. However, there were a few occasions I caught Darren making snide comments to Josh, like: 'Oh, your father would do that.' Well, as you can imagine I was all over that like a lioness. As soon as the boys were in bed there would be a fuming row. He could do what he wanted to me, but I would not stand for that.

Jack was a good kid. He was strong-willed and funny, but still close to me and very loving. But as he moved up through high school he started playing truant from lessons more often than he was in them. And unlike Josh who preferred to keep his head down, Jack didn't seem to care about getting caught. Like any decent mother, I wanted him to go to school and do well for his future, but Darren made me feel like I was making mountains out of molehills. He was so anti-establishment that he found it funny Jack was wagging lessons.

'The boy's got a strong spirit,' Darren laughed. 'I'm not breaking it.'

His attitude was that it was the school's job to keep the kids there. We would get letters home and Darren would hide them from me. When the school sent people round to speak to us face to face, Darren would get confrontational with them.

'So what?' he'd say. 'So what if he doesn't go to school? What are you going to do about it?'

I'd spent so many years with Darren's rigid opinions that I would always be questioning and second-guessing myself. *Maybe he's right,* I'd think. *I wagged school. Maybe it doesn't really matter that much.* It never crossed my mind that this behaviour might be down to Darren's violence, although I know very differently now.

As well as struggling to keep Jack in school all day, Darren and I were called into school to discuss an incident. Jack had been running up some steps where he shouldn't have been and a teacher grabbed him by his bag to pull him back. The bag had been over one of Jack's shoulders and where the teacher had pulled it had left quite a nasty welt on his neck. Darren wouldn't normally have come, but when he saw the mark he was furious

We had a big sit down with the head teacher, Mr Shlick.

'No teacher has got the right to pull a kid down the steps by their neck,' Darren stated angrily.

The head smiled.

'Don't fucking smirk at me!' Darren snapped, riling up in his chair.

My mouth fell open as Mr Shlick smiled again. I knew Darren wasn't the easiest parent to be talking to but why would you add fuel to the fire?

Darren was on his feet now, leaning over the desk and pointing right in Mr Shlick's face. Using the tip of his giant finger, Darren jabbed him in the nose.

'Darren!' I shouted, 'Sit down!'

Mr Shlick was shouting to his colleague on reception now, 'Call the police, call the police!'

Unsurprisingly, not long after we got home we got a phone call from the station and had to go in and give statements. This would have been fine, except Mr Shlick now claimed Darren had punched him square in the mouth!

Darren was charged with assault and we enlisted the help of Gareth Driscoll again who did a fine job of cross-examining Mr Shlick when we all ended up in court.

'Can you tell me what happened?' he asked the head.

'Mr Williams leant over my desk and punched me.'

'Where exactly did he punch you?'

Mr Shlick pointed to his top lip.

'Can you tell me what happened immediately after this alleged "punch"?'

'I recoiled in my chair. Mr and Mrs Williams left. I made a cup of tea and took two paracetamol.'

'And you could drink the tea, Mr Shlick?'

'Yes.'

'Do you know what the word "recoil" means, Mr Shlick?'

'It means to go backwards.'

'So you're saying that a six foot seven man weighing twenty-three stone punched you in the lip so hard that you recoiled from the force, then drank a hot cup of tea. Were there any broken teeth? A split lip maybe?'

It was pretty obvious from looking at Darren that even the lightest punch would have knocked Mr Shlick's teeth clean out. The court obviously agreed as the case was thrown out of

Magistrates Court. For once, Darren hadn't been the bad guy. Well, not completely anyway.

After that any respect I had for the school was gone. How could I trust the head teacher to be a good role model for my kids?

Unfortunately, Jack's truanting got so bad that he was asked to leave high school a year early. We arranged a place for him on a computer course at college and it turned out to be the best thing we ever did. I don't know if it was the change in scenery or that he was treated differently by the adults there, but for some reason he took to college much better than school. We felt like he'd finally turned a corner.

Chapter Fourteen

> *To My Rachel,*
> *So glad I met you*
> *God only knows where I'd be now without you*
> *That thought makes me sick to the core of my stomach.*
> *14 years my love!*
> *Love you with all my heart*
> *Your Darren*
> *xxxx*

In starting to mentally prepare myself for the day I left Darren. I didn't know when, but I knew it would happen and I knew I would be OK. I was resilient and more than capable of surviving without him. The question was: could he survive without me?

In 2010, Darren's sisters and I decided to book a big family holiday to Spain. Their mother had remarried and moved out there to live, which was basically an opportunity for a free holiday. I was still always trying to instigate things with Darren's family, such as meals out and ice-skating at Christmas, but all Darren did was slag them off. He didn't know why I was bothering but I went ahead and booked the flights. Jack and Josh agreed to come, with Josh even asking to bring Emma, a girl he was seeing. We all knew what Darren was like, but with so many of us going, it felt like there would be safety in numbers.

Meanwhile, my sister Nat was getting married. Although I still saw my family regularly, any function that meant inviting me *and* Darren would pose a problem. There was no fall-out as such, but Darren and my mother had never seen eye to eye. He certainly never had a good word to say about her and they hadn't spoken for a long time.

It was Nat who broached the subject with me.

'Listen,' she said, 'I don't want to cause friction, but Mum said she's only coming if Darren doesn't.'

This wasn't ideal, but I could hardly blame my mother for wanting to avoid Darren when I spent my life doing the same. I agreed that Mum had to take preference.

When I told Darren he wasn't invited, his response was: 'I didn't want to fucking go anyway.'

I hoped he would let me go without him but he turned it into an ultimatum.

'If you go,' he said, 'you're sticking up for your mother and you don't give a fuck about me.'

As much as I wanted to stand up to him, I knew there was no point. There was no way I could go now – I couldn't go against his wishes and risk him turning up on the day. He wouldn't give a shit about ruining my sister's wedding.

Our holiday to Spain was in August 2010. The morning we all met at the airport everyone was in good spirits, except for me, of course. I was responsible for everything – money, passports and hire-car information. I had to pack everyone's things – even

Darren's – and couldn't relax until the bags had been checked in. I knew if they were overweight it would be my fault and there would be a showdown in front of the whole airport. Thankfully, we checked in with no problems and headed up to the airport bar. After one or two drinks, Darren and I both took a diazepam to calm our nerves. He had always been a nervous flyer and over the years it had rubbed off on me too. Once we were safely in the air I took out my purse and bought everyone another drink. After paying the air hostess, I had to quickly pull my tray down to take the drinks. I knew if I didn't do it fast enough that Darren would have shouted at me and belittled me in front of the whole plane.

With everyone happy and settled, I closed my eyes to relax and fell into a deep sleep. As well as the diazepam, I think I was exhausted by the early start and the stress of getting to the airport. I was so out of it I didn't wake up until we landed at Murcia.

I grabbed my bag and we made our way off the plane. The second we got outside and felt the glorious sunshine, Darren was beaming. We trotted off to get our luggage then to pick up our hire car. It was in that moment that my mind flashed back to buying drinks on the flight. My stomach hit the floor. I hadn't put my purse back in my bag. I rummaged around in my handbag, praying it would be in there. But it wasn't. I could feel myself burning up. My purse had an envelope in it containing all £550 of our holiday money. Darren was going to be livid.

I grabbed his sister Rachael by the wrist.

'What's wrong?' she asked, concerned. 'You're white as a sheet.'

I whispered to her frantically, 'I think I've left my purse and all the holiday money on the plane.'

Rachael knew as well as I did how Darren was going to react and, judging by the look in her eyes, she was panicking too.

'Darren?' I called as calmly as I could. 'We've got a problem. I've left the money on the plane, but I'm sure it's fine. It'll be found while they're cleaning for the next flight. I'll go and let someone know.'

But before I could leave, Darren erupted.

'You dopey fucking slag!' he roared. 'What the fuck do you think you're playing at? You stupid fucking cunt!'

I ran back to the flight desk to have them radio the plane but it was too late; the plane had already left. I felt sick. I had to walk out of the airport and face Darren, who was now in the car park being calmed down by the men in our group. The second he saw me he knew it was bad news. He threw a bottle of water at me and went absolutely berserk. His eyes were red and bulging with rage and spit had gathered at the corners of his mouth. I was crying and pleading with him.

'It'll be OK!' I shouted. 'We've got insurance! It'll be covered!'

But whatever I said made no difference. He had lost his mind.

Darren started swinging for me. As I backed away, Rachael stood in between us screaming at him to calm down. There were airport staff and holidaymakers everywhere. Darren's younger sister Becky and her kid had been locked inside their hire car by her partner and were now sat watching in tears. Josh was trying to comfort his girlfriend who barely knew us and was freaking out. When Darren saw the state she was in, he bellowed at her, 'Get in the real world!'

Rachael's partner Wayne eventually managed to talk Darren down and get him into his hire car, leaving me to travel with Rachael, Jack, Josh and Emma. As we pulled up at Darren's mum's and got out of the car, Jack said to me under his breath, 'If you don't leave Da when we get home you're an idiot.' He'd heard me threaten to walk plenty of times, but this was the first time he actually told me to do it.

I had hoped the journey would give Darren a chance to calm down, but as soon as we were inside his mum Barbara's house he started again. She wasn't standing for it, though.

'If you're going to start you can leave,' she said.

Darren, being the stubborn pig he was, stormed off, taking one of the cars and spending the night on the beach. As horrible as it sounds, nobody was bothered. It was a pleasure to be able to settle in and relax without him.

The next morning everyone was sat round Barbara's dining table when we spotted Darren's car parked up on the dirt track outside. He was sat there, looking at the house and sulking like a child. We all had a bit of a joke about it, 'oh here he is' sort of thing. When he plucked up the courage to come inside, he was very sheepish. I think he realised that everyone felt sorry for me and that all he'd done was isolate himself.

I never did leave Darren after that disastrous start to our family holiday to Spain. He was an absolute angel to me for the rest of the time we were away, despite some awkward bickering among his family. I let his behaviour slide for the sake of the holiday, but I could feel I was coming to the end of my sanity. Yes, I had lost the money, but I hadn't done it on purpose. I did not deserve the dressing down of the century in the car park of the airport. I put on a smile for everyone around me, but inside I was feeling more and more angry, more and more resentful. I couldn't be a better wife than I was. I couldn't try harder than I was already. But it was never enough. There was always something and it was doing irreversible damage to the last shreds of patience I had for Darren.

Nat's wedding – held the month after Spain – was another reason for my bitterness. I had barely any friends and this was a very stark reminder that Darren was always coming between me and my family too. I got Nat a card and put some money inside. I also bought her a little angel good-luck charm that she could carry on the day and know I was thinking of her. I was gutted I couldn't go but she understood – it wasn't worth the grief.

After Spain, the boys refused point blank to come away with us ever again and I couldn't blame them; if I had my way I wouldn't be going anywhere with Darren either. But in 2011, Brian and Ann invited us to Tenerife. Darren accepted on our behalf and I had no choice but to comply. One morning over a lovely breakfast at our apartment, Darren started. I can't recall the full conversation, but it was about me not agreeing with something he had said in front of Ann. Embarrassed, I stormed off down to the beach to get away from him. I was crying my eyes out with shame and anger, wondering what the hell I had done to deserve a man like this. Before long, Darren caught up with me. He chucked a fistful of sand at me and snatched my bag.

'Give me some fucking money,' he spat.

He took a wad of cash from my purse and threw the bag back at me. I thought he was going to leave but he marched over to a sun lounger a few feet away and just lay down. I stared out to sea, trying to ignore him and collect my thoughts. After about 20 minutes, he came stomping back over – not to apologise *to* me, but to demand an apology *from* me. If I wasn't so shocked I would have laughed in his face. Later that night I told Ann this was the last time I was going on holiday with Darren. And I meant it. I was starting to feel like my life was flashing before me. I was 39 years old – almost 40. The thought of being with Darren for the rest of my life was starting to weigh heavily on my mind. I imagined all the years ahead of me, of being retired and still being with this man. He said he wanted to get away from it all, move to the countryside and live out his days just me and him. This filled me with dread. Granted, he might well be better off isolating himself from every person on the planet bar me, but I couldn't think of anything worse.

I started to ask myself what I would miss about Darren if he wasn't around and struggled to think of anything. I thought of all the times he had hurt me and belittled me in front of people, the violence, all the years I'd spent bending over backwards to please him. When we lay in bed together I found myself wishing he'd have a heart attack or just stop breathing in the night. I knew I couldn't go on like this. I felt a strength coming over me that I'd never felt before. It was the strength I needed to leave.

Chapter Fifteen

I had been in charge of our finances since the day we moved in together. I knew what was coming in and what was going out, and if Darren wanted money he had to ask for it. I thought I was in control – of this aspect of our lives at least – but Darren had played me like a fiddle. By handing me the financial reins, he relinquished all responsibility. He had flipped it to his advantage so the onus was always on me. If Darren wanted money for steroids, weapons or a dog, I had to find the cash no matter what. On more than one occasion I found myself drawing out money using my credit card because there wasn't enough in the bank and I knew he wouldn't accept no for an answer. The control had been his all along.

On Friday, 8 July 2011, Darren called me up going ballistic because I had his bank card. He called me every name under the sun because he needed it desperately and it was my fault he didn't have it, completely forgetting he had given it to me himself so I could pick something up for him. On any other day I would have bitten my tongue and tried to smooth things over. But today, something inside me snapped at the injustice and I started shouting and swearing back. Seething with anger and frustration I cut off the call, knowing just how much it would infuriate him. I was so mad I didn't care. He tried calling back several times but I refused to pick up.

I called his sister Rachael in tears.

'Don't go home,' she said. 'Come to mine.'

She invited me in, poured me a large gin and tonic, and let me cry it out until I calmed down. Once I'd got my head together I had to go and clean the doctor's surgery. Darren kept calling but I was still too furious to pick up. When I finished cleaning, I drove round for hours, unable to go home because I knew Darren would be there. The bank card had been such a minor thing to fall out about, but after the way he behaved in Tenerife I had been waiting for an opportunity to make my move. Was this finally it?

When my phone rang again I assumed it would be Darren, but when I looked at the screen it was Rachael.

'Hello?'

'Rach,' she replied. 'Darren's taken an overdose.'

We had been here so many times with the suicide threats that I almost knew it was coming. I didn't ask her what tablets Darren had taken or how many. I didn't feel sorry for him or like I needed to rush to his side and comfort him. I felt numb. He had used suicide threats to manipulate me so many times that I didn't care he'd actually done it. In fact, once Rachael told me Darren was in the hospital I was relieved because this was my chance to go home.

When I arrived at the house Jack was the only one in. I sat him down and told him what his dad had done. Sadly, Jack knew his dad so well that he wasn't at all surprised.

'Listen, Jack,' I told him. 'I've had enough. I'm going to leave him. I'm going to leave your dad.'

Jack laughed. He had heard it all before.

'I mean it this time,' I said. 'I'm leaving tomorrow.'

That night, the boys and I locked the front door from the inside so if Darren came back he would not be able to get in. Well, not without a fight anyway. I went to bed and lay staring at the ceiling, bracing myself for his return.

I must have nodded off because I woke up to Jack standing over me.

'Mum, Mum,' he said. 'He's outside. He's knocking the door.'

'OK,' I said, sitting up. 'Let him in.'

Darren had taken 12 diazepam. That amount probably could have made a regular-sized person quite ill, but they barely touched Darren because of his size. He had been discharged on the basis that he would be issued a follow-up appointment with a psychiatrist. Groggy and ashamed, he lay down on the sofa and slept it off.

The next morning, I had to be up early. One of my clients was off to a wedding and had asked me to do her hair. When my alarm went off I took a few deep breaths and went downstairs. Thankfully, Darren was still asleep. I made myself a coffee and went back up to get ready. Ten minutes later I heard the familiar thud of his footsteps coming up the stairs. *Here we go*, I thought. My heart was pounding so hard I thought it might jump out of my chest.

Darren flung the bedroom door open and stood at the end of the bed. He looked confused and vacant. His eyes locked on mine as he started pacing backwards and forwards like a caged animal.

'Don't fucking look at me!' I blurted out, half angry and half terrified.

'If you don't like it,' he growled, 'do something about it.'

'I will,' I stated. 'I am. This time you have done it.'

I stormed past him and fled downstairs, through the living room and out the kitchen door. I needed to get outside, to breathe some fresh air. I stood on the back doorstep, my eyes so full with tears I couldn't see the garden properly. Then I felt him behind me, breathing down my neck.

'What the fuck are you going to do?' he laughed menacingly.

'I'm leaving you,' I said, trying to control the fear in my voice. I turned to face him, looking him in the eye. 'I mean it this time.'

In that split second, something told me he knew I was serious. The realisation sent his anger soaring and his face morphed into pure evil. I turned on my heels and headed straight back inside. I did not want to stick around to see what happened next. But before I could make it through the living room Darren was behind me, his hands locked around my throat. He was shaking me violently, squeezing, strangling. My legs buckled and we both fell to the floor as I gasped desperately for air and clawed at his huge fingers. His grip was so tight it felt like my neck might snap. For the first time, I felt like he had lost control of himself. *This is it,* I thought. *He's going to kill me right here on my living-room floor.*

The boys burst in. Jack was holding up a baseball bat and Josh was holding his mobile phone. On his way downstairs he had quickly dialled 999. He didn't speak to the operator – there was no time – but he left them on the line hoping they would hear what was going on and send help.

'Get off her, Da!' Jack shouted.

Darren heard and instantly released his grip. I leapt up off the floor and in one motion slammed my fist down on the top of his head. I don't know where I got the strength or courage, but I felt I was fighting for my life.

For a few seconds, Darren seemed dazed by the blow. Then the tears came.

'I'm so sorry,' he cried, burying his head in his hands. 'Rachel, please don't do this. Please don't leave.'

The boys went back upstairs to their rooms. They knew that, when Darren turned on the waterworks, things had calmed down and 'Daniel' was on his way back. Only this time, Darren wasn't finished. With his eyes still puffy and red, he grabbed me by the arm and started dragging me upstairs to the bedroom. I didn't understand why at first – surely he could just do whatever he wanted to do in the living room? Then a light came on in my mind: after all the years of threatening suicide, I had this really strong feeling he was going to slit his wrists in front of me.

Darren pulled me round the bed to his side of the room. He had one hand clamped around my wrist trying to contain me as I struggled. With the other hand, he was trying to reach inside the drawer on his side of the bed – the drawer where he kept his knives.

I suddenly noticed that he was fading. He looked tired and was out of breath, probably still woozy from the overdose the night before. I managed to break free and back away onto the landing.

'Oh no you don't!' I screamed in anger. 'You are not going to do that in front of me!'

Jack came out of his room.

'What's he doing?' he asked.

'Go on then!' I screamed at Darren. 'Slash your wrists in front of your sixteen-year-old son!'

I shouldn't have said it, but I thought it would shame him into not going through with it.

I ran downstairs, only to hear Jack's voice as I reached the bottom step.

'Oh no! Mum! He's done it!'

The day Darren strangled me and then slit his wrists was a huge turning point in our story. We both knew that I meant it when I said I was leaving. Why else would he resort to trying to end his life in front of his teenage son? He was desperate. He was having to resort to lower and lower tactics to try to get what he wanted. Only it wasn't working; I was done. The fear of staying had become greater than the fear of leaving.

When Jack shouted to tell me what Darren had done, I didn't rush upstairs to help him. I walked through to the conservatory and sat down calmly. I winced as I touched my neck, which was sore from where Darren had choked me just moments earlier. I closed my eyes and tried not to move. In that moment, I hoped that he would bleed to death on the bedroom floor and be gone from our lives forever.

Meanwhile, Jack was making two calls: the first was for an ambulance, the second was to Rachael, who arrived just before the paramedics. I simply sent everyone upstairs to deal with Darren. When two young coppers came to the door, I did the same.

'He's upstairs,' I said, letting them in.

As they disappeared up to the bedroom I pulled the collar of my dressing gown up around my neck and started walking to the conservatory to sit back down. Before I'd even got to my seat, I heard Darren addressing the police at the top of his voice.

'Get out of my house! Just fucking get out of here!'

Seconds later I heard their footsteps coming back downstairs. One of them poked his head in on me and said: 'You all right?'

I looked at him as if to say, 'Do I look all right?' But the only words that came out of my mouth were: 'I'm fine.' And with that, the police were gone.

Darren refused to let the paramedics take him to hospital, agreeing that Rachael and Wayne took him instead. Once he was out of the house, I spent the day packing his things. I never made it to do my friend's hair. I was in such a state I don't think I even rang her to cancel.

After a day at home resting, I started my week back at the salon. Once he was discharged from hospital, Darren went to stay with Rachael. He didn't call or text. For now he was leaving me alone – another well-worn tactic for when he knew he was in the dog house but working towards winning me round. What he probably didn't bank on was that his actions that day had only reinforced my decision to end the marriage and get away from him. Although things were far from over, for now, at least, me and the boys could go about our daily lives without the fear of a bad mood or violent outburst. I was getting a taste of freedom and the life I had been longing for.

Jack chose to maintain some contact with his father, which I respected. He even took to looking after Darren's dogs for him. Josh felt no such loyalty, and I was adamant that I didn't want to know a thing about how Darren was doing or what he was up to. It was easier to be strong that way. I had big plans and I didn't want anything getting in the way of them.

On Wednesday, 13 July, five days after Darren strangled me, I did something I had never done before: I went to see a solicitor. Her name was Michelle and she was wonderful.

'I want to divorce my husband,' I told her.

'OK.' She nodded. 'Can I ask why?'

Well, as you can imagine, I gave her plenty of reasons. I told her everything and she agreed to get the ball rolling right away. This was a huge step forward for me, but I chose to keep it to myself for now. I knew my friends and family wouldn't believe I was finally leaving Darren so I decided to wait until things were further along. I wanted them to know that this time I meant business.

By this time Darren was back in touch, trying to call and sending texts telling me he loved me and couldn't live without me. Jack still loved his dad, but he would read the messages and laugh.

'He's so pathetic, Mum,' he said. 'He's like a kid. He needs to grow up.'

I tried not to get sucked into Darren's games, keeping any contact brief and to the point. 'You can live without me,' I told him. 'You will get over it. Life goes on.'

Things turned nastier when he didn't get his way, with Darren saying I wouldn't get a penny from the house if I left him. I knew he was just trying to hurt me because of how much pride I took in our home. But I couldn't have cared less about the house by this point. If it was going to be the thing that held me back, then I was happy to sell it and cut all ties. I was so focused on my future that me and the boys went and viewed a two-bed flat in the nearby Maplas area. They said they were happy to share a bedroom and we kept it in mind as an option.

The week beginning 18 July, Jack told me Darren was planning to come home.

'He says he's coming home this Sunday,' Jack said. 'You've got to move out or he'll make you take him back. Th said he's going to play head games with you and make you love him again.'

I knew I had to start making plans. I arranged to move in with Sue, a girlfriend of mine, where I knew I could keep a low profile. She had a council house so I was only allowed to stay for two weeks without being declared as a lodger, but I told her that was all I needed. I packed up the things I wanted to keep for my new life and put them safely away in storage. Jack and I decided that I would make my escape in plenty of time in case Darren tried to trick us by coming home early. So on Saturday, 23 July we got up at 4.30am. Instead of packing my clothes I just pulled out all my drawers and put them straight in the boot of my car. The boys wanted to stay at home together until we settled on a place for the three of us to live. I never felt they were in any danger from Darren, so I agreed. It was only me he wanted.

For the next two weeks I stayed at Sue's, meeting up with the boys most days to give them money, food or any other essentials they needed. It was also a way of making sure we were all OK. I don't know if Darren had a clue where I was, but as far as I know he didn't come looking. Jack told me he had gone back to work now he was well enough, which was music to my ears. If Darren was out at work, I had even more freedom to arrange not only the divorce but also the sale of the house.

My solicitor Michelle felt that I should consider giving a statement to the police about the strangling on 9 July. I wasn't sure if I wanted to push things that far. Surely it would only antagonise Darren if I reported him? But she felt that it would strengthen our case if the incident was on record. I was so torn I ended up confiding in my friend Nikki, the policewoman. She knew what Darren was like and how hard it was for me to consider this, but she managed to convince me to go to the police.

So on Monday, 25 July I nervously took myself down to Gwent Police Station and gave a statement. I did this on the understanding that I was accusing my husband of a serious crime and that the wheels would then be set in motion for him to be arrested. It wasn't easy, but I knew it was the right thing to do. Now the police had all the facts, I'd done my bit. It was time for them to do theirs.

They said my case would be passed on to the Serious Violent Crimes team and they would need statements from Josh and Jack to back up my claims. Josh agreed. He wanted to support me and do the right thing. Jack, however, was more conflicted and decided not to – he didn't want to be complicit in condemning his father to a prison sentence. This upset me, but I didn't want to force either of my boys to do something they didn't want to do. We were going through enough as it was. In the end, the statements from Josh and myself were enough for the police to want to charge Darren with assault.

The same day I gave my statement I had a valuation done on the house while Darren was out at work. I paid to have an energy certificate done, then gave the go-ahead to put the house on the market. I'm not sure how I managed it because, legally, Darren had to sign all the paperwork too. But somehow it all went ahead, no questions asked.

I was anxious for word from the police but heard nothing for days. I made several calls to them, but no one could tell me when Darren was going to be arrested. They said that, because of his previous firearms offence, his size, and the fact he was so outspoken about his hatred for the police, there was talk of using an armed response unit to make the arrest.

We were in August now and Darren had received the paperwork for the first stages of our divorce through the post. He told Jack he had no intention of signing. When this got back to me, I rang the landline, told Jack to put me on speaker phone and screamed at Darren to sign it or else. But it was the news that I'd put the house up for sale that got to him the most. He phoned me in a state saying he'd driven home from work to find the For Sale sign outside.

'I can't handle this,' he cried. 'It's all happening too fast. Please don't do this. I love you, we can work it out.'

'Give it time to sink in,' I said coldly. 'We'll split everything fifty–fifty. I don't want a fight. I just want all this to be over.'

Everything *was* happening fast. I was steaming ahead at 100 miles an hour because I was afraid that, if I stopped, I might crumble and go back. I couldn't allow that, not this time.

When Darren tried calling me again, I ignored him. He started leaving messages begging forgiveness, pleading with me to reconsider. Some I listened to, some I just deleted. I'd heard it all so many times he was like a broken record. I could feel myself getting stronger and stronger. I was moving forward without him pulling on my heartstrings. I was detaching myself, not just physically but emotionally too. His grip on me was finally beginning to loosen.

Chapter Sixteen

After two weeks in hiding and with the divorce and the sale of the house now fully in motion, I decided I needed a blowout. I called my sister Nat and told her we were going out.

'What? Shopping?' she replied, confused.

'No!' I laughed. 'A proper night out! Me and you!'

'You're having me on,' she said.

'I'm deadly serious,' I said. 'I've left him. I've started divorce proceedings and the house is up for sale. Now are you going to take me out for a drink or what?'

Nat was shocked but by no means surprised. At this point she probably still believed that I would end up going back to Darren eventually. But for now, at least, she was delighted to hear that I was so far forward in my mission to break free.

We agreed to meet that Saturday and that we would go to Cardiff as there would be less chance of bumping into Darren or anyone who knew him. My belly fizzed with a mixture of excitement and nerves – it had been years since I'd been out on the town on my own. But once I was all dressed up in a brand-new jumpsuit and getting a lift into the city, I felt a million dollars.

It was a hot summer's evening and all the bars were heaving. The first pub we went in was so full I felt a little overwhelmed. Nat went to get us a drink while I scanned the room. I was suddenly aware of a girl dancing next to me. I started to feel like she was a bit closer than she needed to be. I smiled at her and tried to back away a little, only to spot two girls across the room snogging each other's face off.

'Guess what?' Nat shouted over the music as she handed me my drink. 'Two double gins for seven quid!'

'Nat,' I replied, leaning into her ear, 'I think we're in a gay bar!'

'I don't care where we are,' she laughed. 'If it's seven quid for two doubles, we're staying!'

We had a good giggle at our rookie mistake, finished our drinks, then decided to try somewhere else. We settled down somewhere a bit quieter, only to get approached by two young lads who were clearly trying to chat us up.

'Listen, boys,' I said gently. 'We're having a girls' night. We're not really interested in anything else.'

'Is it because you're married?' one asked, clearly a little wounded.

'How old are you?' I asked him.

'Twenty-one,' he replied proudly. He was only a year older than Josh!

'I am literally old enough to be your mother!' I laughed.

They soon skulked away and, as we headed back outside, I started to feel a little flat. The bars we'd been to weren't really doing it for me. This wasn't shaping up to be the big night out I had imagined.

Then, I had a light-bulb moment.

'I know! I'll text Gar! He'll know where to go!'

Gareth was the solicitor Mum worked with, the one who represented Darren. He was a family friend and still lived in

Cardiff. If anyone knew where to go it would be him. It had been ages since we last spoke, but I texted him on the off chance he still had the same number.

'What are you doing out?' came the reply. Everyone knew I wasn't allowed out without Darren.

'I've escaped!' I texted back. 'I'm divorcing him.'

Gar then rang my phone and gave us a few options of where to go, but our enthusiasm had dwindled.

'Well, if you don't like my suggestions,' Gar said, 'you could always come to mine?'

Nat and I jumped at the offer, grabbing the next taxi we saw. Gar lived in the middle of nowhere, somewhere between Cardiff and Newport. His house had a long driveway with large gates that we had to buzz for him to open. Once inside, we heard his dogs barking and saw chickens and ducks milling around.

'This place is amazing!' Nat exclaimed.

Gar opened a bottle of red wine and poured us both a large glass. I stole one of Nat's cigarettes and lit up. Darren was so anti-smoking that I hadn't touched one since I got pregnant with Jack and he was 16 now. I don't know why I did it but it felt amazing. I felt liberated. For the first time in 18 years I was doing whatever the hell I wanted.

The three of us sat drinking and chatting until 2am.

'I should be getting home,' Nat said, looking at her watch.

'OK,' I agreed. 'We've imposed ourselves on poor Gar enough for one night!'

We called a taxi then made our way outside to wait for it. With Nat walking ahead of us, Gar pulled me back and started to kiss me. It took me completely by surprise, but I found myself kissing him back.

The taxi arrived but, just as I was about to get in, I said to Nat, 'I'm staying.'

Then I turned to Gareth and said, 'Is that OK, Gar? Do you mind?'

'Of course not!' he smiled.

'You're not staying!' Nat said.

Laughing, I told her I was. She rolled her eyes and admitted defeat. We waved her off then went back inside for more wine. One drunken thing led to another and I woke up the next morning in Gar's bed. Oddly, I didn't feel any guilt. I had been faithful to Darren for all these years, regardless of what he did to me. I felt that now we were over I'd more than earned the right to do what I wanted. Spending the night with Gar was a giant leap forward for me. The very last of the emotional ties had been cut and it was full steam ahead.

With my two weeks at Sue's coming to an end I had to think about where I was going to go next. I finally told Mum and Colin that I was leaving Darren and they offered me a bed at their place, which I gladly accepted.

Over the next few days I checked the progress of the divorce proceedings and found we were still waiting for Darren to sign the paperwork. He was refusing to cooperate, so my solicitor Michelle was in the process of writing to the court to let them know what was going on.

It was close to two weeks since I had made my statement and Darren still hadn't been arrested. The police kept telling me they couldn't locate him, that he was working away and that things were simply taking longer than expected. I made calls; my mother made calls. Every time we rang we spoke to somebody different. With every day that went by I became more and more anxious for my safety. I felt like a sitting duck.

Then, on Monday, 8 August, Jack told me that Darren had taken another overdose.

'It was a big one this time,' he said, 'He's in the hospital.'

I tried to sound concerned for Jack's sake, but we both knew this was another cry for help in the hope I would go running back. I thought the police would arrest Darren now they knew where he was, but still no arrest was made.

Darren was released from hospital on the Wednesday – his birthday of all days. He started calling and texting me. The messages were mostly incoherent ramblings, I guess because he was still all over the place from the overdose. But the bottom line was he wanted to see me.

'What kind of state is your father in?' I asked Jack.

'He can barely walk properly, let alone talk,' he said.

With that in mind, I felt this was my chance to tell Darren for the last time, to his face, that the situation was real and our marriage was over. I had to make it clear to him that no matter how many times he tried to take his own life I would not be going back to him. So, just after lunch I drove back to our house and let myself in. The boys were upstairs on their gaming consoles and Darren was asleep on the settee in his pants. There were a couple of birthday cards and gifts – I assume from his family – on the floor next to him.

'Da, wake up,' I said. He stirred and came round.

'What do you want, Da?' I asked.

'You,' he said. 'I want you. I can't live without you. Just take the house off the market and move back in. I'll get a flat to give us some space. We can take things slowly. I'll see a counsellor. I'll get all the help.'

I let him finish then watched in calm silence as he crawled over to me. He was at my feet now, pleading with me. I felt like our roles had reversed – I was the one in charge. He could see by my stance that I had no pity for him now.

Darren got up and went out through the kitchen to the downstairs loo. I went to get a glass of water and could see him sat on the toilet, crying, unshaven and slurring his words. This is what he had become. Nothing he said would ever change my mind now. And once this realisation sank in, it didn't take long for Darren's temper to make an appearance. He came out into the kitchen shouting, thumping his chest and punching his head.

'I can't take being me any more! I can't live with being me any more!'

I took this as my cue to leave. As I turned and walked out the door, Darren screamed at the top of his voice: 'I can't live without you!'

I turned back to look at him one more time.

'Well, guess what? I *can* live without you!'

I ran to my car and just cried and cried. As strong as I'd been about leaving Darren, it was still really distressing to see him in such a terrible state. I didn't want to be with him, but I didn't want this. I called Rachael and begged her to help.

'He's in a really bad way,' I told her. 'I can't cope with this any more. I can't help him. I don't know what to do.'

'Rach,' she said. 'You have to do what you have to do. We will look after him. But you need to know something. The girl you were staying with is telling everyone you slept with Gareth. I don't know if it's true or not. I guess it doesn't matter. But there are people who know – close friends of Darren's – that want to tell him.'

My heart was in my throat. *How could Sue do this? She knows Darren will kill me if he finds out about that night.*

'Please,' I begged Rachael, 'tell them to think about what they are doing.'

'I'll do my best,' she said. 'But he's going to find out somehow. Be careful.'

I put down the phone, panic rising in my chest. I couldn't believe that a friend who knew everything about Darren, a friend I had trusted 100 per cent, was spreading the news about me and Gar. She knew all about Darren's persistent threats on my life and how he would react if I even looked at someone else. I had no idea why she would do this to me.

Then it hit me: this was my death sentence. In the euphoria of leaving Darren, starting the divorce and selling the house, I had been strong. But now all the years of verbal threats were back in my head. *I can't live without you … the only way you'll leave is in a wooden box.* I suddenly felt helpless and overwhelmed. I couldn't do this any more. What was the point in fighting when I was never going to win?

It was in that moment that I decided to take my own life. I picked up some tablets and a bottle of wine and drove to a beach in West Wales around an hour and half from home. I sat staring out to sea thinking, *This is it. This is the end of the road for me.*

I've got nothing left. I knew that, if I didn't kill myself, there was a good chance Darren would do it for me. He'd said so to my face more times than I could remember. I felt so empty and afraid. All the pressure of trying to do this on my own had finally got the better of me. I just wanted peace. And surely a quiet death on my own terms would be better than a brutal end at the hands of Darren?

Chapter Seventeen

Something happened to me that day as I looked out to sea preparing to die. Just when I was about to give up, I felt a surge of anger and strength. I looked down at the pills in my hand and thought: *Rachel, what the hell are you doing? You have kids! And a life!* I was not going to let Darren drive me to this. I was going to face the bastard head on.

I started the car and drove back to Newport like an absolute lunatic.

On the way, Jack rang. 'Mum, Da's gone crazy. He's smashed the TV. He said he's going to kill you and Gar.'

Darren knew I'd slept with Gareth. He'd been told by Rachael's husband Wayne and a friend, people who thought I'd been out of order and that Darren deserved to know regardless of the consequences.

'Don't come home,' Jack warned. 'Go to a hotel or something. He said he's going to kill you and he won't be going to prison either.'

I knew exactly what that meant. Darren would rather die than go back to prison. He wanted to kill me and then himself.

I called Mum and told her what was happening. She rang the police and Gar to warn them Darren was on the warpath then called me back.

'The police said to go straight to Central Police Station.'

I had my foot to the floor and was not going to stop for anyone. When I got to the police station I slammed the brakes on, abandoned the car and practically threw myself inside. Mum and Nat were already there.

'The police are out looking for Darren.'

'And Gar?'

'He's safe.'

An officer called Jody took me upstairs to a private room where I had to give a new statement. By now it was dark and close to midnight, but it was such a hot night the windows and blinds had been left open to keep the room cool. We hadn't been talking long when we heard an almighty commotion outside and then a man's voice.

'Where the fuck is she?' it boomed. 'If she's here I'll fucking kill her!'

It was Darren.

'I'm just going to go and see what all the fuss is about,' Jody said, getting up and leaving the room.

I sat there, terrified. Yes, there were walls, locked doors and police officers everywhere, but Darren had size and strength on his side. I knew what he was capable of and I did not feel safe. The noise went on for several minutes as I sat listening and trembling about him. Eventually, when it all went quiet, Jody came back. She was white as a sheet.

'He's big, isn't he?' she said. 'I've never seen anyone the size of him before.'

Darren had apparently been picked up by the police, on his way to see Gareth, I assumed. I shudder to think what might have happened if they hadn't caught up with him. But instead of taking revenge on Gar, that night Darren was finally charged with assaulting me – 15 days after I reported it. He was kept locked up for around 48 hours until his court appearance on Friday, 12 August.

I stayed away from the hearing but was told afterwards that he had pleaded not guilty to common assault. This wound me up because he was such a stickler for the truth. He was always demanding it from everybody else and yet he didn't have the balls to admit what he'd done.

I had hoped he would be remanded in custody, but with the next court date not till 24 October, Darren had been granted bail. The terms were that he lived with his sister Rachael; that he adhered to a curfew from 6pm until 6am; that he did not come within a three-mile radius of the marital home; and that he did not contact Josh or Jack as they were both potential witnesses in the case. I would have felt safer if he was under lock and key, but at least he was on the radar now. I felt the police were finally taking us seriously and, with the bail restrictions providing some peace of mind, I now had the option to move back home with the boys until we sold the house.

Before I could move in, there was a lot of cleaning up to do. The day Darren found out about me and Gar he had rampaged through the house like a tornado, putting his fist through our 50-inch TV and throwing it across the room. The seat had been ripped off the downstairs loo and he had taken chunks out of walls. The boys said it was like he was possessed. The place was a mess, but it was no less than I expected.

I stayed at Mum's and went to work as normal, although I was careful to alter the times I cleaned the doctor's surgery in case Darren did come looking for me. It was a small measure, but one I felt better taking nonetheless. In my spare time, I went back to the house to clean up and move my belongings back in. I did a food shop as Darren had not bought groceries since I left the house and, bit by bit, I started to put all his belongings into black bags and move them outside to the shed.

It was while sorting through the clothes in the bedroom that I noticed something strange about my wardrobe. I'd not been in it for weeks as there were clothes in there that I hadn't needed, and yet when I opened the doors the metal rail looked rusty. Then I noticed the hooks on the hangers were rusty too. I wondered if I could smell bleach, only to find an empty bottle of it discarded near my feet. It was then that the penny dropped. *He's thrown bleach all over my stuff.* Loads of my things were now ruined, including a pair of black leather boots that I loved. I didn't know exactly when Darren had done this, but I knew it was him. I got straight on the phone and reported it to the police.

During this same week, Jack told me Darren had been going to the gym. The gym was only a mile away from our house so he was breaching his bail conditions by being there. I rang the police to make sure they knew this, and so did my mum. We wanted everything to be on record now.

The police arranged for me to have a security system fitted by a locally funded organisation called the Bobby Van scheme. On Thursday, 18 August, they came to the house and spent half a day reinforcing the doorframe of my bedroom and installing multiple locks on the inside. It looked hideous, but if Darren got into the house I would be able to use the bedroom as a kind of panic room. They also installed a black box with a panic alarm that I could press in an emergency, and police would be there in minutes as a matter of high priority.

All this provided me with some much-needed reassurance. However, that same day, I got a call from the police saying Darren had been back to court to challenge his bail terms. The police were fuming because they hadn't been notified and the magistrates had allowed almost all the restrictions to be lifted. The only terms now in place until the court case on 24 October were that Darren stay at Rachael's and keep away from Brynglas Drive. I didn't understand. How could Darren be granted more lenient bail when he had broken it by going to the gym and pouring bleach on my clothes?

All I could do was try to keep my head together. Darren was still out of the way, the house was as safe as it could be, and the police had everything under control. I told myself I wasn't going to let Darren's silly mind games get the better of me.

I went back to Mum's to get the very last of my stuff and told her that, now my room had been made safe, I would be sleeping in my own bed. She looked sick with worry.

'Rachel, love,' she said, 'why don't you just stay here?'

But I'd made up my mind.

'No, Mum. I'm not running any more. What's the worst he can do – kill me? Well he'll have to kill me.'

Chapter Eighteen

That night I slept in my own bed for the first time in six weeks. I took some comfort from the security measures that had been installed at the house by the local Bobby Van scheme, but I still had a nagging sense of foreboding over what Darren would do next. As long as he was walking free, I knew he was a threat.

Although I didn't usually work Fridays, on 19 August I got up and went to Carol Ann's to cover a shift for a friend. I didn't know it yet, but that morning, as I saw to clients and chatted about the glorious weather, Darren was hunting me down. He was a man scorned, ready to take matters into his own hands.

At 2.20pm he made his move. When he appeared in the doorway of the salon I knew that he had come for me. I tried to stop him when I first saw the glint of the silver shotgun. I screamed at him to stop, to think of Jack. But he struck me in the forehead, knocking me backwards onto the floor. Before I could get up, he stretched out his arms, pointed the gun right at me and shouted: 'I love you, Rachel!'

I curled up into a ball just as he pulled the trigger. I felt a blow to my left knee and a strong smell of gunpowder filled the air. I looked down to see a hole in my jeans. There was a watery orange liquid but no blood and I don't remember any pain. The reception telephone was now on the floor next to me. I reached out and made a clumsy attempt to dial 999. Then came the second bang. I felt the blast whoosh past the side of my head. There were more screams and an even stronger smell of gunpowder.

Darren was crouched down now, picking up his bag. My eyes instinctively searched for the gun – he had put it on the floor and, I assume, was about to reload. This was my chance. I lurched forward making a beeline for the weapon. I somehow managed to grab it, but Darren wasn't about to give up now. We grappled for a few moments, but what chance did I have against a man possessed – a man more than twice my size? I was thrown backwards again, Darren's boots and fists pummelling down on me until I was as lifeless as a rag doll. He fled the scene – I believe – thinking I was dead. Part one of his mission was complete.

The next thing I remember is a man crouched at my side.

'Can you hear me?' he said. 'Can you tell me your name?'

'I know who I am,' I murmured. 'I'm Rachel Williams and my husband just tried to kill me.'

Anita was putting a towel under my head and saying anything she could to keep me talking.

'Don't go to sleep,' she pleaded gently. 'I need you to do my hair!'

A paramedic appeared. 'You might feel a sharp scratch,' he said. The morphine entered my system and everything went black.

As I slipped in and out of consciousness, my memory of what happened inside the ambulance is hazy. I was taken to Royal Gwent Hospital in Newport and placed on a high-dependency ward. The lighting was dim, I think, and there were people fussing over me as I continued to slip in and out of consciousness.

I recall a nurse saying, 'You are so lucky to be here. Point-blank range with a sawn-off shotgun? Not many would survive to tell the tale.'

The first familiar face I remember seeing was that of my godmother Mary, who worked at the hospital as a cleaner. News of the shooting had reached that side of my family almost immediately. Although the details had been sketchy, my real dad Stewart heard there had been a shooting at Carol Ann's, and, instantly fearing for my safety, rang my half-sister Sandra. Sandra alerted her mum, Mary, who was able to navigate the hospital and get to me reasonably quickly. I kept asking for my phone because I knew people would be trying to get hold of me.

'Here,' Mary said, pressing her mobile phone into my hand, 'there's plenty of credit on there. If you need to ring anybody you can.'

Back in Newport, news of the shooting was spreading like wildfire. The solicitor's office where Mum worked was just a mile and a half away from the salon. Like a lot of the shops nearby, they went into lockdown the minute they heard there had been an incident. Mum had a feeling of dread in the pit of her stomach telling her that this was her worst nightmare coming true. Hearing that the incident was at Carol Ann's was all the confirmation she needed. She couldn't get to the hospital fast enough.

Natalie told me later that she was at home when her husband took a call from the police. When he relayed to her that I had been shot by Darren, she screamed, 'I knew he would do this!'

The police warned Nat to stay away from the hospital. Darren was still at large and they were concerned for the safety of anyone closely associated with me. Not knowing what else to do, Nat fled to the house of a friend that Darren didn't know and waited anxiously for more news.

Meanwhile, I was lying in hospital with a police forensics team taking photographs of the injuries to my left leg. In the middle of my forehead, next to my hairline and in line with my nose, I had a huge lump where Darren hit me with the butt of the gun. As we were moving, I remember the paramedic wrapping a bandage around my head and saying, 'I've been doing this job twenty-odd years and I've never seen a lump like this.'

I recall one of them telling me, 'Your husband is still on the run. We're doing everything we can.'

I knew Darren did not want to go back to prison. I knew his plan that day had been to kill me then kill himself. I assured them they would not be finding Darren alive.

Unbeknownst to me, the hospital was crawling with armed police in case Darren showed up. Another officer was heading to Brynglas Drive where he would knock on the door of our house and break the news to my sons. Within an hour or two of the shooting they were stood by my bed, taking in what Darren had done to me. Jack was white as a sheet and Josh was in tears. I was so pumped full of morphine that even though they were right next to me they seemed really far away. I remember Jack saying quietly, 'I didn't think he would do it, Mum.'

Our visit came to an abrupt end when I got taken into theatre. I was put to sleep while surgeons washed out my leg and fitted an external frame to hold everything in place. This was a temporary measure to get me stable while they figured out what to do next. When Mum heard I'd been shot in the leg but that I was alive, she imagined a small hole where the pellet had hit. But while I was under she and Colin were warned that my injuries were extremely serious and the prognosis for my leg wasn't good.

When I came round I was back on the ward. The boys were gone but Mum and Colin were still there. Nat was in the chair next to me now too, fear and worry etched all over her face. Despite the warning from the police, she had been physically unable to stay away any longer. I had an oxygen tube up my nose and was hooked up to a machine that topped up my morphine automatically. My ear had been alarmingly swollen from the beating and while I was in theatre a surgeon had to keep making slits with a surgical knife to release the build-up of blood. I think he had to do it seven times in all. Someone came in to ask my permission to use the shotgun pellets from my leg as evidence. I agreed; I was hardly going to keep them as a souvenir.

Now the doctors had had a chance to assess me properly, they were able to explain what damage Darren had done. The gunshot had blown my left knee to bits. The bone loss was massive and the patella tendon, which attaches the bottom of the kneecap to the top of the shin bone, had been all but obliterated. I lay there listening to the surgeon, high on morphine and amazed we were even having this conversation. While he was talking, I was wiggling my toes and moving my left foot backwards and forwards.

'Look!' I said pointing at my foot cheerily. 'It's not broken!'

'Rachel,' he said, 'I'm really sorry. I have to warn you – there's a high chance we'll have to amputate.'

'No way!' I said, almost laughing. I couldn't believe what I was hearing. 'There must be something you can try?'

The surgeon smiled meekly. 'I had a feeling you'd say that. We're going to transfer you to Swansea tomorrow morning. They might be able to do more there.'

With all the drugs and the goings on I had barely given Darren another thought. But around 8pm that night, with Mum, Colin and Nat still at my bedside, two police officers arrived.

'Mrs Williams,' one said, 'we've got some news about your husband. I'm afraid he is no longer with us. We understand that he has taken his own life. It would appear that he has hanged himself.'

Everyone's eyes were on me, waiting for my reaction. I felt a surge of emotion mushroom upwards through the morphine – relief, elation, euphoria. I opened my mouth and the most astonishing noise came out. 'Yeeeeeeeeeeeeehaaaaaa!' I screamed. 'The wicked witch is dead!

Chapter Nineteen

I always knew there was going to be some serious comeback for filing for divorce and sleeping with Gareth. But despite all the times Darren threatened to kill me, I could never in my wildest nightmares have anticipated he would show up at the salon with a shotgun and shoot me in broad daylight. I expected him to have more consideration for his son than that. But now, as I was starting to digest what happened, I could see that there was only one solution in Darren's mind. His plan was to kill me so no one else could have me, then kill himself so he didn't go down for my murder. He ran away from Carol Ann's that day and hanged himself from a tree in the woods, believing I was dead.

I appreciate that my reaction to Darren's suicide may seem a little out there. What you have to remember is I knew deep down it was coming. And the moment it came I knew I was finally free. I didn't have to leave him now. I was never going to be running away or looking over my shoulder. In a way, he had made it easy for me.

And another thing you have to remember is that I was completely off my trolley on painkillers. To emphasise just how out of it I was, it didn't even enter my head to call my sons to tell them Darren was dead. However I felt about his suicide, if I was in my right mind my first thought would have been to console

Jack over the loss of his father. But I was literally away with the fairies. It was night-time and things were winding down at the hospital. The police left, the nurses made me comfortable, then I just slept and slept and slept.

The morning after the shooting, the nurses got me ready for my transfer to Morriston Hospital in Swansea. When I was wheeled out to an ambulance, I passed a police officer, completely unaware he was there because of me. Because of the nature of what happened and because my story was now national news, the hospital had me logged under the alias Jane Doe. Again, I had no idea about any of this.

Nat was by my side for the 50-mile journey which took well over an hour. When we arrived, I was still so high on the drugs I started waving at a man with a black eye.

'Oi!' I shouted. 'I've got a black eye too!'

He laughed and gave me a thumbs-up.

At Morriston, Nat took photographs of my injuries. We agreed it would be good to keep a record in case we needed it for any reason. As well as the main gunshot wound to my leg, I was heavily bruised from the beating Darren gave me after I tried to grab the gun. There were so many bruises we kept finding news ones. On my back, there were some in the shape of Darren's finger marks. I itched my arm and realised it was tender, only to find another bruise in the shape of his boot.

I asked Nat to get me a mirror so I could see how I looked.

'You sure?' she asked nervously.

'Yeah, I wanna see!' I said.

She found one for me and I looked at the woman staring back. The lump on my forehead was so big it was comical. Both my eyes were black; well, more like purple and yellow at this point. The bridge of my nose was puffy and tender and there was a bruise on my neck that went right down to my collar bone.

'You OK?' Nat asked.

'I'm fine,' I assured her. And I meant it. I was alive. My nose was still intact. I didn't have brain damage. Sure, I didn't look pretty, but after everything I'd been through I wasn't going to fret about a few bruises. The elation I felt at being completely free from Darren far outweighed any concerns about my health. I wasn't wallowing, I was thanking my lucky stars. I was so upbeat that it freaked everyone out.

Sometime during my first few days at Morriston a mental-health worker came to see me.

'Hi, I'm Ron,' he said. 'I'm a mental-health nurse. Can I come in?'

'Yeah, come in!' I said cheerily, gesturing him over to the bed.

'I've come to see how you are. How are you feeling?'

'I feel great!'

Ron explained that he was worried my euphoria over Darren's death was not reasonable behaviour. He said it could be down to shock or that it might be a symptom of a deeper problem or disorder such as bipolar. I told him everything: what Darren was like; the mental-health issues, the violence, how pity and fear stopped me leaving.

'So, tell me, Ron,' I said when I was done, 'how would *you* feel if your husband had tried to kill you? How would *you* feel if you survived and he didn't? Wouldn't you be euphoric if all that was over?'

'Do you know what?' Ron said. 'The way you've just explained everything, I feel like you've answered all the questions I came in here to ask you.'

As the news of Darren's suicide sank in, my thoughts naturally turned to his funeral. It was bizarre given the circumstances, but as Darren's wife I felt that, whatever I thought of him and however I felt, it was my responsibility to organise things. I wasn't sure how I was going to manage it, physically or financially. I didn't even have any intention of attending, but I felt that the job of making the necessary arrangements naturally fell at my door. So when Darren's sister, Rachael, got in touch and asked me to sign all the rights over to her, it was a weight off my shoulders. I was more than happy for a member of Darren's family to take over and organise the ceremony as they saw fit. Rachael's partner Wayne brought the paperwork to the hospital and I gladly signed everything they needed to proceed. We also agreed that they could borrow Darren's Land Rover so they had a vehicle for the funeral.

Over the course of that first week I had my injured leg washed out three times. This was a painstaking three-hour-long process to remove dead tissue and debris, and minimise the risk of infection. I was introduced to the wonderful Mr Mullins – a very experienced surgeon with extensive knowledge of leg injuries. His plan was to operate using titanium rods to rebuild my leg. Unfortunately, the parts he wanted were only available in America so we had to play the waiting game until they arrived.

Mum and Colin were backwards and forwards to the hospital every day. I remember Josh coming, but not Jack. This was strange because we were so close, but he sent text messages instead saying he loved me and was praying for my leg. I thought maybe he had found it too hard seeing me in the hospital, especially knowing that his dad was responsible for the state I was in. He also had the second blow of losing his dad to deal with, so at this point I was happy for him to do whatever felt right.

My sister Natalie refused to leave my side, sleeping in the chair when she couldn't keep her eyes open any longer. I couldn't get rid of her. We got my phone back from the police and slowly went through all the missed calls and messages. Just about everyone I knew had tried to get hold of me the day of the shooting. There was a message from Sandra who, after hearing I had been shot, offered to pick me up and take me for a drive to get me away from Darren. We laughed about it when she came to see me but at the time her head had been all over the place with panic.

The get well soon cards and bunches of flowers poured in. Nat had to find some Blu-tac and stick the cards up on the walls as there wasn't enough space to stand them all. Inside the cards were messages of love and support from family and friends, people I hadn't seen in years, even people I didn't know!

We got wind that my local paper, the South Wales Argus, wanted to speak to me, but I had no intention of doing anything like that. I didn't really see the point of it. However, I did start to realise just how big my story was to the outside world; ITV Wales sent me a huge double-layered box of Thornton's chocolates. I remember this because I was eating very little at the time as the antibiotics I was on had killed my appetite. I kept looking at the box thinking, *One day I'm really going to enjoy eating you!*

The titanium parts for my legs finally arrived, and on Friday, 26 August, exactly a week after the shooting, I was wheeled into theatre for my big operation. Mr Mullins had warned me that there was no right way to do things. There was so much damage that any surgery and subsequent treatment was going to be all about trial and error. I had lost 60 per cent of my patella tendon and there was extensive tissue and bone loss, not just to my knee but my shin bone too. In places, the bone had been reduced to nothing but dust. Miraculously, not one single blood vessel had been hit, which was why I hadn't seen much blood in the salon.

Mr Mullins and his team carried out a full knee replacement. Because I'd lost so much tissue, they then used part of my calf muscle to rebuild the leg around it, taking a skin graft from my thigh to patch everything up. They worked on my leg for ten hours while Mum, Nat and Colin sat drinking canteen coffee and biting their nails with worry. A nurse told them that she had never seen so many boxes of parts in the theatre.

Apparently, most people are sick when they are coming out of anaesthesia. When I came round, the first thing I asked for was a cup of tea and a biscuit. I guess I am not most people! The op had been a success, but only time would tell just how well my leg would recover. Our main concern now was keeping any kind of infection at bay. A gunshot drives all the surrounding dirt and material into the wound, which in this case was mostly denim from my jeans. An infection could develop at any time and derail my whole recovery.

The day of my operation, the *South Wales Argus* ran an interview with Darren's mother, Barbara. My family saw it because everyone was following every last shred of the coverage.

Nat kept a copy for me to read when I was up to it. The headline was: *MALPAS ROAD SHOOTING: Gunman's mum – my heartbreak*. Barbara talked about her pain at losing a second son to suicide and told the paper that Darren had never recovered from his brother's death. She said: 'I would never deny that what Darren did was very shocking. Darren was no angel, and what he did was terrible but on the other hand he was no brainless thug. He wasn't this big brute people were saying.'

The article brought snippets of new information to light for me. It claimed that before the shooting Darren was seen at the cemetery where his brother was buried. I believe he went there to say goodbye or 'see you soon'. Darren had also called his sister Rachael and her partner Wayne to tell them both he loved them. He sent a text to Wayne too, saying: 'To take revenge is often to sacrifice one's self.'

Barbara said that, when she heard about the shooting and that Darren was missing, she was praying he wouldn't kill himself. They all knew as well as I did what his plans were and what he was capable of. While I sympathised with Barbara's grief, it didn't feel right to be saying 'poor Darren'. I had stood by her son for 18 years, trying to hold him and our family together, and he had turned up at my place of work to kill me. I was still lying in the hospital battered and broken, and if he were alive he would be facing an attempted murder charge! I stared at the pictures of Barbara posing with Rachael and Wayne. They had even got Jack to do the shoot with them. No one had asked me if I was OK with him being in the paper and I wasn't sure I was. I started to wonder if I should speak to the *Argus* myself. After all, it was me they wanted: maybe I should give them my side of the story.

Unfortunately, while I was in the hospital focusing on my recovery, secrets were being kept from me. Josh was staying at Brynglas Drive and leaning on my mum and Colin for support. Jack however was not coping well. The day of the shooting, when he came to visit me in the hospital, Mum found him in the toilets texting Rachael to come and pick him up. At this stage, we didn't know Darren was dead and Mum was understandably desperate to keep the boys safe.

'You need to stay here,' she told him. 'Your father's on the loose.'

'He's not going to fucking shoot me, is he?' Jack snapped angrily.

'Well, he shot your mother!' Mum replied. 'Be under no illusions what he is capable of.'

After the news of Darren's suicide broke, Jack decided that he wanted to stay with Rachael and Wayne. He would eat and sleep there overnight then nip back to ours for a shower and change of clothes. All this had seemed reasonable to Mum and Colin at first, but they soon started to feel unsettled by some of the things that were going on. For example, Josh told them that, when Jack was nipping home, he had started bringing members of Darren's family into the house with him. Josh felt uncomfortable about this and didn't see the need for Jack to have an escort in his own home. But when he tried to confront his brother, Jack was angry and defensive.

It's hard to pinpoint exactly when I realised something was up, but I remember Josh coming to see me and looking stressed out.

'What's wrong, love?' I asked.

'It's Jack, Mum.'

'What do you mean?'

'He's being a twat, Mum. If he carries on I'm gonna slap him.'

This didn't sound good. Jack liked to wind Josh up for a laugh sometimes but I could tell this was different. Something wasn't right, but my head was so all over the place I just couldn't put my finger on what.

Darren's funeral was arranged for 30 August, just after the Bank Holiday. Josh had absolutely no intention of going, which was perfectly understandable to me but upsetting for Jack, who felt Josh was disrespecting his father. It was heart-breaking to hear that they were falling out now, right when they needed each other. I wanted to sit them both down, give them a hug and tell them everything was going to be OK. But I was stuck in the hospital. I tried to contact Jack but got no reply. Then I got a random text saying he had been to see Darren at the morgue. I wasn't happy about this – I didn't feel it was healthy for a 16-year-old boy to see his father in that way, especially given that Darren had hanged himself. Surely that would be upsetting for Jack? But no one had consulted me and there was nothing I could do now he'd been.

In that same week, with my operation out of the way, I decided to go ahead and speak to the local paper. Nat made the call and I gave an interview over the phone. I told them that Darren had been violent to me for years and had done this because I was in the process of leaving him. I told them I knew that he would try to kill me then kill himself to avoid jail. I expressed my concerns about the system because I desperately tried to get help for Darren on numerous occasions and could never seem to get any. I also wanted answers as to why bail restrictions that were put in place by the court to protect me were then lifted. I didn't know why this had happened and why on earth I wasn't notified.

Before the story even ran, things between me and Darren's family suddenly took a turn. I was just having the bandages taken off my leg when out of the blue, Darren's sister, Rachael – who I had always been close to – sent me a text calling me a black widow. She said she knew everything about me and Gar and that I had blood on my hands. I couldn't believe what I was reading. She knew better than anyone what Darren was like.

It came to my attention that there were rumours flying around that me and Gareth had been more than a one-night stand. In what I can only imagine was a nasty case of Chinese whispers, people were now claiming we had been having an affair for three years! This complete fabrication seemed to be what was fuelling Rachael's venom towards me.

I'm not going to lie – I replied to Rachael's texts and I didn't hold back in defending myself. It was now crystal clear to me that Rachael – and probably the rest of Darren's family – were twisting anything they possibly could to take heat off Darren and push blame on to me. Terrifyingly, this meant that my grieving teenage son was living with someone who had a vendetta against me. I was under the impression Jack was having counselling and that he had enough family around him to keep him safe and supported until I got home. How wrong could I have been …

you're nothing but a fucking slag. It's all your fault Dad's dead.

Jack's words, fired at me in an angry text, cut like a knife. The loving boy who climbed into bed with me every morning would never speak to me like that; not in a million years. It confirmed to me that his head was being filled with disgusting lies. I knew he always sided with the underdog – maybe he thought Darren was the underdog now? Darren's family certainly felt that way. But why was everybody turning on me when it was Darren who did this? I'd never felt more helpless. I desperately needed to see Jack.

The *Argus* published my story over two days, using the photographs that Natalie took. I was happy with the piece, but it prompted another text from Rachael, calling me a 'fucked-up wife and mother' and saying I didn't deserve my kids. This was rich given that her mother had spoken to the press to defend her son, while allowing mine to be pictured in the paper days after his father's suicide. Surely I had a right to tell my story? And again, it just confirmed Rachael was trying to turn Jack against me. She had been perfectly nice to me when she wanted to take control of Darren's funeral. Unlucky for her, this backfired because the rest of the family were furious she had taken charge. With the family at loggerheads and having to hold two separate wakes because Darren's parents couldn't be in the same room as each other, Rachael was then lumbered with a funeral bill for thousands of pounds that she couldn't afford.

On the back of my speaking to the *Argus*, a journalist called Jane who worked for *Wales News* came to the hospital and left some flowers and a card with her number. I was feeling riled up by the lies being circulated about me so got Nat to give her a ring. She was dealing with so many calls from journalists we joked that she was like my new PA.

Jane said she wanted to interview me and write a feature for a women's magazine. This would be written in my own words in more detail than the local paper. I told Nat I wanted to do it: everyone was talking about me whether I liked it or not, so why not put everything out there?

'I've been silent for too long,' I said. 'I'm not going to shut up about this now. I want people to know everything.'

Jane – a rockabilly with black hair and red lips – came to see me and took notes from my bedside as I opened up even more. Something was motivating me. People were interested in my story and I wanted to shout it from the rooftops. With Darren out of my life for ever, there was nothing holding me back now. I'd put up with his behaviour for too long, believing his tears and making excuses for him. As I opened up to Jane, I was finally starting to realise that maybe I had been in an abusive relationship all along. And if this could happen to me, it was happening to other women like me, women who might not even realise what they're experiencing.

Meanwhile, tensions at home were getting out of control. Someone had broken into our shed and taken some belongings of Darren's that I bagged up before the shooting. A laptop was missing, and then Scooby was stolen. Someone had forced their way into the back garden and taken him. Josh was going out of his mind.

I had been in hospital around three weeks when Jack cut his wrists. For Mum and Colin this was the straw that broke the camel's back. They had kept me in the dark about a lot of things to protect me. They knew how close Jack and I were and how distraught I would be that he was acting the way he was. But things were now so serious that they knew they had to tell me what was going on.

'I'm so sorry, love. We didn't want to worry you,' Mum said. 'It feels like he's out of control. We just don't know what to do.'

The exact details passed on to me were vague – I don't know where he did it or who he was with – but I cried imagining what a mess his head must be: his mum almost murdered, his dad strung up on a tree in the woods, everyone telling him what a bitch I was. It was a lot for any of us to take in, but for a 16-year-old boy? No wonder he was all over the place.

Desperate to speak to him, I called his mobile over and over. Sometimes it rang, sometimes it went straight to voicemail, but he never picked up or replied to my texts. I felt helpless. All I could do from my hospital bed was make phone calls – so that's what I did. I called Social Services hoping they would provide some help or advice but was told that because Jack was 16 there was nothing they could do. I tried CAMHS (the child and adolescent mental health services) and told them that whatever follow-up counselling Jack was having after his father's death and now his own suicide attempt would be undone the minute he was back in that toxic environment with people who hated me. Mum tried to reassure me that the cuts to Jack's wrists were minor and it was just a cry for help. I wanted to believe her, but in the days that followed his behaviour only seemed to deteriorate further. He not only ignored my attempts to contact him, but refused to speak to Mum, Colin and even Josh. It was like we were split down the middle – my family were supporting me, and Darren's were grieving for him. Poor Jack was slap bang in the middle. He loved his dad, but was struggling to come to terms with his father shooting me and then killing himself. For whatever reason – comfort, support, I'm not sure – Jack chose Darren's family over mine. Sadly, I believe his choice was heavily influenced by other people's lies and opinions about me.

Mum wrote Jack a letter. Out of worry and desperation she put pen to paper because she could see no other way of saying what needed to be said. In the letter, she assured Jack that yes, he might feel hurt and bereft now, but things would get better with time. She told him that she and Colin were only a phone call away and that they loved him very much. Jack responded by texting me: 'Tell Nan thanks for the letter, but don't send any more.' Again I tried calling and texting, but got no further replies.

Not one to give up, Colin kept checking on Josh and the house, making his presence known. During one of his checks he found himself face to face with Jack who had turned up at the house to get some stuff. He wasn't alone: he had brought Wayne and Richard – one of Darren's friends – with him. Colin just wanted to ask Jack what was going on. Was he OK? Why was he refusing to speak to us? But with Wayne and Richard there to back him up Jack was on the defensive from the get-go. Things escalated quickly, insults were thrown at Colin, and Jack spat at him. It pains me to write this so I can only imagine how distraught Colin was. My half-sister Sandra pulled up in her car just as things were kicking off. She screamed at Jack, Wayne and Richard to back off and got straight on the phone to the police.

Life for my family was spiralling out of control. As if they weren't having enough worry with Jack, someone superglued the locks on Mum's car and my front door. Nat had the locks on her car glued shut and one of her tyres slashed. We were constantly in touch with the police who were backwards and forward to take statements every time something happened. We even had a death threat made on the landline while the police were sitting in my living room. When Darren died I thought my nightmare was over, but it was only just beginning.

Chapter Twenty

During my recovery at Morriston Hospital I was never short of visitors. All my old friends turned up. Tayrne, Dan, and Claire Brian and Ann came. I tried to put people off because the hospital was such a long way from Newport, but nobody listened. They would all ring first to see if I needed anything picking up and they would car share to save on fuel costs. At one point I had all three of my dads – Colin, Ray and Stewart – wanting to visit. It was like performing a military operation so none of them would bump into each other. Even now I can't believe how many visitors I had. It was overwhelming.

My half-sister Sandra was always popping in to see how I was. We talked about Darren a lot and she knew everything that had been going on in Newport since the shooting. During one visit she asked me something completely unexpected.

'Rach,' she said, 'did Darren have another son?'

'You what?' I said, shocked. 'Nah. No way. What makes you say that?'

'Oh, just something I saw on Facebook. I might have got it wrong. I just wondered if you knew.'

I didn't give the conversation a second thought at the time. Darren told me everything; there was no way he had a kid before he met me and never told me. And there was no way on earth he would have had one behind my back. Darren was a lot of things but he wasn't a cheater.

As each day ticked by – a blur of visitors and physio – the more anxious I became for Jack's well-being. I was so far away – too far for him to come alone on a bus. Because I could no longer count on speaking to Jack myself, I contacted the police in an attempt to nip things in the bud. I told them Jack was to either be at home with Josh or stay at Rachael's. He couldn't be going back and forth between the two like he was. With all the stuff going missing and the fact Jack always had someone else with him, it was causing too much stress for Josh and my family. I tried to be diplomatic, saying that if Jack really wanted to stay at Rachael's that was fine. I knew how headstrong he was and I didn't want to add more fuel to the fire by giving him an ultimatum. But if Jack did decide to stay at Rachael's, I wanted the police to take his house key off him so I could guarantee some security for Josh and our things. The police assured me that all this sounded perfectly reasonable and that they would speak to Jack as soon as they could. I really hoped Jack would see sense and choose to be with his big brother, especially now I was getting ready to go home.

I couldn't have asked for more from the people who took care of me in hospital but by the end I was desperate to get out of there. I was sick of the food, of being bed-bound staring at the same four walls, and, more than anything, I needed to see Jack.

An occupational therapist came to assess me and made arrangements for things I would need at the house – a wheelchair, a Zimmer frame and a commode. I was offered a stair lift but I told them to get stuffed.

'I won't be like this for long!' I said.

It was just over five weeks since the shooting when my doctor offered to discharge me.

'You have everything you need at home now,' he said. 'How do you feel about being discharged?'

I wanted to say yes so badly. I'd been paying into a payment protection plan for years so I knew my earnings would be covered and I would be OK financially, but my injured leg still felt so fragile that I decided to stay a few more days. It was Friday, 23 September – five weeks after the shooting – when I finally agreed to let them turf me out. With my bandages and brace still on I was told I could not put any weight on the leg until my first outpatient appointment in two weeks' time. I was given a pair of crutches to help me get about. Nat came to pick me up so I was put in my wheelchair and rolled out to her car. Because of my injury and the cumbersome brace I had absolutely no bend in my left leg, which meant we had to slowly manoeuvre me into the back so I could sit with my leg stretched out across the back seat. It wasn't the most comfortable drive of my life but it was such a relief to finally be out of the hospital. However, any relief was overshadowed by a sense of trepidation that hung over me every time I thought about Jack.

On the way to Brynglas, Nat and I passed a Burger King. I wasn't much of a fast food or burger fan, but after all the tasteless, grey hospital food something about that restaurant called out to me that day.

'My taste buds are telling me I need a burger, sis,' I said.

'Burger it is then!' Nat smiled, pulling into the drive-through.

So I wouldn't have to go through the rigmarole of getting out and back in again, we ordered the food and stayed in the car to eat. I demolished that burger in seconds and on that day, in that moment, it was hands down the best thing I had ever tasted.

We continued the drive home where we knew my half-sister Sandra would be waiting for us to help Nat get me out of the car. One of my neighbours had very kindly lent us a wheelchair ramp to help them wheel me into the house. As I shuffled awkwardly out of the car and into my wheelchair I was suddenly aware of people around me.

'Rachel? What's it like to be home?'

It was the press. They had got wind I'd been discharged, and rushed to the house hoping for a comment. Even though I had given two interviews, they were still hungry for more. After five weeks in hospital it was a bit overwhelming to have them right in my face. I put my jacket over my head and Nat and Sandra got me safely inside. Speaking to reporters was not my priority.

I arrived home to colourful 'welcome home' banners, not just at my house but on some of the neighbours' houses too. All the get well soon cards I'd received (there were over a hundred in the end) had been transferred to my living room and placed on display. Nat and Sandra had really gone to town.

'I couldn't wait to see your face!' Nat laughed.

'I know,' I said. 'I'm a bugger for cards – if it was up to me they'd be tidied up and put away by now!'

'Listen,' Nat said, 'we've got a few people coming round tonight. We've arranged a little welcome home party for you.'

The drive home had been so exhausting I wasn't sure I felt up to it. All the trouble everyone had gone to was incredibly touching, but all I could think about was the fact Jack wasn't there to greet me. I could not remember a time I had been away from home and he hadn't been there to do that. But the party was organised whether I liked it or not. Nat and Sandra laid on the food and drink and it didn't take long before people started turning up to get a look at me. I couldn't drink because of the painkillers and antibiotics but Mum arrived with a big hug and a bottle of alcohol-free wine. It was wonderful to see so many faces – old friends like Alex and Jayne who Darren referred to as slags until I gave up spending time with them. I was so grateful to know that after everything they were still my mates. Carol from Carol Ann's came with her daughter, my next-door neighbours Linda and Rachael. Poor Claire decided not to come. She'd had people turning up at the branch of Tesco where she worked and making threats – all because she was a friend of mine.

Pretty much every conversation that night centred around where people were when Darren shot me. I started to feel like bloody John F. Kennedy! But after being cooped up for so long dealing with my injuries, it was eye-opening to get a sense of how everyone else's lives had been affected too.

I chatted to a neighbour of mine who confessed that the first time she ever saw me I had been running down the street trying to get away from Darren. She had watched him catch up with me and drag me back to the house by my hair.

'I'm sorry,' she said. 'I had no idea how bad things were.'

The crazy thing was there had been so many incidents like that I couldn't even remember the time she was referring to.

When Brian and Ann turned up, Ann told me that when she saw the state of me in the hospital it took everything she had not to burst out crying. They were shocked by the way I looked, but less so by what Darren had done. They knew him so well that they almost knew it was coming. Ann also told me that Darren had been up to see them when he found out about me and Gar. They said he was like a wild animal, pacing about and punching the air with spit coming out of his mouth. He told them I was nothing but a slag and that I'd always taken the piss out of Ann behind her back. Thankfully, they didn't believe a word of it. Ann sat flicking through a magazine refusing to engage with Darren while Brian – a tall man but in his late sixties – tried to reason with him.

'I thought I was going to have to rugby-tackle him at one point,' Brian said.

They presumed he must be off his head on medication and from the way they described him I think they were right.

Around nine o'clock there was a knock at the door. We assumed it was another guest, but it was two policemen. I got up onto my crutches and hobbled to the conservatory so we could sit and talk away from the noise.

'What can I do for you today?' I asked.

'It's about your son, Jack. He is saying that he would like us to pick up the rest of his belongings.'

I thought about this for a moment. Of course I wanted Jack to have anything he needed, but I also wanted to sit him down and tell him everything was going to be all right.

'I'm going to have to say no,' I said. 'I'm home now. If Jack wants the rest of his clothes he can come and get them himself.'

The policemen left and the party started to peter out as I wondered how I was going to get upstairs. I looked around at my house, the house I bought and shared with Darren for all those years, and was surprised just how easy everything felt without him. For the first time in years I had no fear. I was home and I was at peace. I hoped it was going to last, but something told me it wouldn't.

Chapter Twenty-One

Over the course of my first weekend back at home, I came across a letter from the police saying that Jack had been arrested for assaulting my step-dad, Colin. I sat open-mouthed as Nat told me about the altercation outside our house and Jack spitting on his grandfather. I was shocked, disgusted and so upset. This wasn't the Jack I knew. I wanted to snap him out of this madness. He was still nowhere to be seen, but I was clinging to the hope that he would soon come back to the house. Surely he wanted to see me? I knew he wanted the rest of his clothes at least.

I'd lost so much weight in hospital that all my clothes were either too big for me or too small to go over my leg brace. On Monday, 26 September Nat and Sandra offered to take me shopping to the nearby retail park so I could look for some wide-leg trousers that would fit easily over my brace. I got out to the car on my crutches and stretched out on the back seat again. As we pulled away from the house and got down the road, I saw a group of Jack's friends waiting at the bus stop. It wasn't unusual for Jack to walk up Malpas Road and meet them all there.

'They must be waiting for Jack,' I said.

I looked at my watch; it was just after 1pm.

Our shopping trip was a success. I found myself some half-decent trousers that fit me and covered my leg. We tried to browse the shops a bit more but it quickly became apparent that I didn't have the energy to shop like I normally would. The girls took me home and made me comfortable. Late afternoon my home phone rang. It was the police.

'Mrs Williams?'

'Yes?'

'It's about Jack. We were wondering if you've seen him today.'

'No, he hasn't been here,' I said.

'He was supposed to meet some friends today but he didn't turn up.'

I thought back to the boys at the bus stop.

'Yeah, I saw his friends down the road, but I didn't see Jack. If I had I would have stopped to talk to him.'

'OK, thank you. We'll keep an ear to the ground.'

'Let me know when you find him.'

'We will.'

I put down the phone, fear rising in my chest. *He wouldn't ... would he?* I turned to Nat.

'Jack was supposed to meet his friends but didn't show up.'

'Where do you think he is?'

'I've got no idea. Let's go and look for him.'

Josh was upstairs in the bath. I stuck my head round the door to tell him what was going on. 'Josh? The police just rang. They can't find your brother. We're going out to look for him.'

'OK,' he said. 'I'll get dressed and do the same.'

We struggled out to the car and set off towards Malpas Road in case Jack might be walking along there. We looked down the lanes, round the back of Bettws, the Fourteen Locks canals centre. We looked until we couldn't think of anywhere else but there was no sign of him anywhere. I tried his phone but it was switched off. My next option was to ring the home of one of Jack's best mates and speak to his mum. She told me I wouldn't be able to get Jack on his phone because he'd recently got a new one.

'Have you got the number?' I asked, crossing my fingers.

'Sure, hold on.'

She gave me the number and I tried it immediately. My heart leapt when it started ringing, but with every fruitless ring, my hope faded a little more. *Where is my son? Is he OK? Why won't he speak to me?* I sent him a text telling him that I loved him and to come home. 'We can work through this,' I said.

My leg was starting to ache from being cramped up in Nat's car. In our hurry to leave the house and look for Jack, I hadn't thought to pick up my medication.

'We need to get you home,' Nat said.

As we drove back to Brynglas I called Josh to fill him in.

'We haven't found your brother,' I said. 'We've tried everywhere I can think of in the car. Maybe you should go and check the woods?'

Brynglas Woods were a few hundred yards from the house. In the summer months when the bluebells came they were especially pretty. Darren used to walk his dogs there and Jack loved to do the same with Scooby. My last hope was that maybe he had gone up there for a wander.

Nat and I arrived home to find the house empty. Josh had gone out to check the woods like I'd asked. I racked my brain for other people I could ring for clues of Jack's whereabouts and decided to try the home of another one of his close friends. Again, I spoke to the boy's mother, who said she had just seen

Darren's sister Rachael and her partner Wayne out checking the woods too. The search for Jack was well and truly on, but my first thought was for Josh's safety. With everything that had gone on, I did not want him coming face to face with Rachael and Wayne. I told her I'd call her back, put the phone down and rang Josh to tell him to come straight home. He didn't answer. I called back the friend's mum to see if she knew any more.

'I don't know what's going on, Rachel,' she said. 'But it doesn't look good.'

'What do you mean?'

'Oh God.'

'What? What is it?'

'Wayne just screamed. He's running. He's running back out of the woods. I think he's found something ...'

Her words hung in the air. I wish I could say I didn't understand what was going on, but in that moment, I did. Jack was missing ... the woods ... Wayne screaming. I put the phone down and I knew. My boy had taken his own life, just like his father had done.

Chapter Twenty-Two

I felt like I was underwater. I could hear what was going on around me but it was like I was listening from deep inside a swimming pool. I could only focus on one thing: the words *Jack's gone Jack's gone Jack's gone* hammering away inside my head like they wanted to split it open. I felt like I was slipping under. Then the sound of screaming pulled me back.

Josh burst through the front door, shouting, screaming and crying. He knew. Nat was reaching out to him, trying to calm him down but he was hysterical. I stood, frozen in shock as he staggered around the room like an animal in distress. He smashed his fist into a door then fled up to his room.

Nat must have called Mum because moments later she and Colin arrived. I remember them both being out in the back garden, sobbing their hearts out as they tried to console each other. Two policemen came to the house to break the news. Knowing everything we'd already been through the past few weeks, even they looked ashen at the latest horror that was unfolding. As soon as they set foot inside the house it was obvious to them that we already knew, but they still had to do their job. Jack had been found slumped on his knees with a rope around his neck. It's believed he lurched himself forward to block his airways, pass out and die from asphyxiation. He didn't do it in the same woods as his father – as the papers would go on to report incorrectly time and time again – but he did it in Brynglas Woods where half of Darren's ashes had been scattered. *Was that why he went there?* I will never know the significance of that, but Jack had researched his method on the Internet before he died.

Everything is such a blur, the noise of tears and distress all around me. I felt like I was stuck in the centre of it all, frozen in a nightmare. There was a sense of blackness, and I was completely numb.

People kept talking about getting a doctor for me, which I didn't understand.

'What do I want a doctor for?' I asked quietly. 'I've just been in hospital for five weeks.'

Apart from those words I barely spoke. I think it was potentially quite alarming for everyone that I wasn't crying and that this was the second serious trauma for me in less than two months. To put their minds at ease, the family doctor came and checked me out. He gave me sleeping tablets, which I didn't take. Well, not that night any way.

I hadn't seen Jack since 19 August, the day of the shooting. I knew immediately that I did not want to see his body. Darren's family liked to visit the morgue two or three times when they lost a loved one. I knew that they did it with Wayne and assumed they probably did it with Darren. But why would I want to look at the empty shell of my son? I wanted to remember Jack as he was.

When I climbed into bed that night, my head began to swirl: why had Jack done this? If he was so desperate, why didn't he come to me, his mother? I could have helped him if he'd just talked to me. I wondered if I'd tried hard enough to reach out to him and get through to him. I went over and over every text and conversation, racking my brain for answers. And all the while I couldn't escape the feeling that there was really only one person to blame in all this. It was Darren who shot me, Darren who tore our families apart, maybe even Darren who put the idea in Jack's head that death was a way out. The tears finally came and I cried and cried until sleep crept in and took me away.

Next morning, I woke early to find the nightmare was still true. Nat and Jayne had spent the night and the kettle was on before I could get downstairs. I found myself on autopilot: arrangements needed to be made for Jack's funeral. I had been happy for Darren's family to deal with his funeral, but this was *my* son. I was going to do it *my* way.

The next few days are a painful and hectic blur. There seemed to be officials in and out of the house constantly. The police were back and forth, the vicar came and I took phone calls from the coroner. I had to decide whether Jack would rather be cremated or buried. The whole time I kept thinking; *I shouldn't be doing this. Jack should be here.*

I don't know exactly when, but someone started making anonymous calls to my house, ringing the house phone and shouting 'murderer' down the line. I was in no fit state to retaliate. If I had then I think I would have ended up in a prison cell. Instead, with Nat and Jayne's help, I logged the calls and reported them to the police. Along with the text messages I had been receiving from Rachael and the petty crime that basically equated to the harassment of my family, I was able to put forward a case for injunctions on Rachael, Wayne and Richard, the friend of Darren's who told him about me and Gar. A police warning was also issued to Richard's girlfriend Mary, who we believe was responsible for harassing Nat. Before this could go through the system, Mum had a brick put through her window. We were in hell.

Nat stayed at the house for a couple of nights until I sent her home to be with her own family. Jayne, meanwhile, refused to leave and moved in full-time. She was like a guard dog, barely sleeping a wink. She would sit downstairs all night, ready to jump on a nasty phone call or to make a note of someone unwanted driving past the house. Every morning she'd hear my crutches clunking across the bedroom floor and, by the time I was downstairs, the kettle would be on and I'd have two boiled eggs and a piece of toast, regardless of whether I wanted them or not. I couldn't have asked for a better friend in a crisis.

I decided I wasn't going to bury Jack. My fear was other people using his grave as a shrine, and me and my family not being able to visit for fear of bumping into them. I hated that these decisions were now motivated by fear instead of choice, but that's what things had come to. I would have him cremated and scatter his ashes in a place that only me and my trusted loved ones would know about.

While I was trying to deal with all these practicalities and decisions, Sandra asked me again whether Darren had another son. I felt pretty sure it was more nasty Chinese whispers – Darren was many things but he wasn't a cheat, but there was clearly something making Sandra wonder. We logged onto Facebook so she could show me some comments she'd seen. If I remember rightly there was a comment from Darren's mother saying something along the lines of: 'Finally glad to meet you.' There was also one from Rachael, saying: 'lovely to meet you, nephew.' These comments were on the page of a girl called Isobele. She had a photograph of Darren as her profile picture and was the mother of a teenage boy who looked around the same age as Jack. Her son's name – of all the names in the world – was Josh. I couldn't believe what I was seeing.

'See,' Sandra said. 'It looks like he had another son, doesn't it?'

'And he's called fucking Josh!'

Any sympathy and understanding I had for Darren's past and his mental-health battles was now gone. In its place was nothing but anger. This man didn't just talk about how bad infidelity was – he would rant and rant about how it was the lowest of the low. Every chance he got he would look down his nose at cheaters and call them the scum of the earth. And to top it all, he had tried to kill me because I'd slept with someone else once when we weren't even together!

When I'd got my head together I rang the police and told them what I knew. I wanted them to investigate who this Isobele was. Did she have some kind of hold over Darren? I knew he would have done anything to stop me finding out about this because it would have been my golden ticket to end the marriage. Most importantly, I wanted the police to tell me whether Jack had found out about Darren's other son. If he had, I knew he would have been crushed. At this stage I couldn't rule out the fact that this might have been what pushed him to kill himself.

It didn't take long for the police to follow this up for me. They paid Isobele a visit and she confirmed it all. She and Darren had an affair and Josh was Darren's son. Darren had even given them financial support, handing over £1,000 when Isobele needed a new sofa. The police ruled out any blackmail and said with confidence that Jack had not known about his half-brother. This gave me some reassurance, but I had other things on my mind now.

Jack's funeral was booked for Thursday, 7 October. There would be a ceremony at St John's Church followed by a short service at Gwent Crematorium. I consulted Jack's friends about the music he would have liked and they suggested the song 'Forever Autumn', which I never would have known about. We also agreed on 'You've Got a Friend in Me', because Jack was obsessed with *Toy Story*.

Meanwhile, the police were still investigating the shooting, focusing a big chunk of their resources on trying to find out who provided Darren with the sawn-off shotgun. They were also trying to keep on top of all the incidents of street crime and harassment that my family and friends were dealing with. There were so many I can't even remember them all, but Josh's girlfriend had the wing mirrors kicked off her car when it was parked outside my house. The police assured us this incident would be on CCTV, but when they obtained the footage it was too grainy to even make out if it was a man or a woman.

For my safety, I was given a mobile phone with a tracker on it so the police would be able to locate me at any time. I was the first person in Newport to have one of these devices. I was granted temporary restraining orders on Rachael, Wayne and Richard, which were now in place, but my mother still felt she had to tell the police in no uncertain terms that we would need a heavy police presence at the funeral. To be honest, with all the hate I was getting there was a point when I only wanted my own family and friends there. Given the tensions between me and Darren's family, and the circles Darren moved in, we knew there were people who wouldn't be holding back just because a teenage boy had died. If anything, they were going to be even more riled up.

I heard on the grapevine that there were plans to do some kind of memorial march for Jack the night before the funeral. I don't know if this was meant as some sort of protest against me, but I couldn't help but interpret it as more anger and bitterness. To their credit, the police acted as go-betweens and managed to get Darren's family to call off the march. I agreed that banning a whole section of mourners would only cause more trouble and, with the police's help, wrote a statement on social media calling for peace and respect, which was liked and shared many times. The police promised us faithfully to our faces that they would be there on the day and measures would be put in place to keep the peace. I went to bed feeling reasonably confident that we could all put our differences to one side, even if it was just for one day.

The morning of Jack's funeral I took some strong painkillers that I knew would carry me through the day. My house was filled with cards and flowers. Josh's friends, dressed respectably in smart black suits, were gathered in the living room. My broken heart felt a pang of happiness that they were making such an effort to support him.

'Rach?' It was Nat. 'The cars are here.'

I got in my wheelchair ready to be pushed outside. I knew it was going to be tough out there. I was going to see Jack for the first time since the day of the shooting and he was going to be in a coffin. Nat helped me out, I closed my eyes and tried to hold myself together. When I opened them, I saw the hearse and the word 'Sparrow' spelt out in flowers. It was beautiful, but confirmation that my boy was really gone.

We had three cars – one for Josh and his mates, one for Mum, Colin, Nat and some other family members, and then mine. I was at the front of the convoy in a car with some of Jack's closest friends and Jayne, who wasn't leaving my side for love nor money. As we drove to the church in silence, I noted the police dotted along the route.

When we arrived at the church, I was taken aback by the number of people outside. It felt like there were people on top of people and I was struggling to make out who was who. Our driver took us round to the side entrance so I would be able to get inside the church using my wheelchair more comfortably. The car stopped and we all got out, with Jayne helping me into my chair. Hardly a word was spoken. I felt the weight of the day bearing down on me.

We entered the church to find it was already full. Jack had been brought in through the main entrance so we made our way to the coffin and lined up in front of it. Josh was by my side with his friends next to him. I clocked a group of people standing behind us at the entrance. As we stood there for a few moments, waiting to walk my dead son down the aisle for the service, a member of this group started shouting abuse at Josh.

'Are you happy now?' someone sneered. 'It's your fault Jack was arrested. Shame on you.'

The tears were streaming down Josh's cheeks. There had obviously been more vicious Chinese whispers about who called the police when Jack spat at Colin. It felt like the whole world wanted to lay blame at our door.

I grabbed Josh's wrist before he could retaliate.

'Not today, Josh,' I whispered. 'Ignore them. This is about Jack.'

I ushered him down to the front where we took our seats. The service started but I was on edge; I could feel the tension in the air. The vicar started to read a beautiful eulogy that Colin had prepared. It talked about how close Jack had been to my mum and Colin, the time they spent together and the special memories they had of him. Out of the corner of my eye I spotted Barbara, Darren's mother. My jaw nearly hit the floor when I realised she was sat with her fingers in her ears. I can only assume she found it hard hearing how close my kids were to my parents, but still – have some respect.

The vicar finished Colin's eulogy and a local girl called Charlotte started singing 'In The Arms of the Angels'. To my absolute horror, some of the so-called mourners started coughing and talking over the song. I turned my head ready to throw daggers at whoever was being so disrespectful, only for mobile phones to start ringing! I was livid, and I wasn't the only one. A murmur of angry voices rippled through the church. The vicar looked frightened. The tension in the room was palpable – something was about to kick off. People were on their feet. A cross bearer ran down the aisle. Jayne decided she was going to get me out of there. I was woozy from the painkillers but, still, I knew my son's funeral was being cut short because people didn't know how to behave. I was fuming that after everything I had not been able to sit in the church and be fully present for Jack's funeral. All I had wanted was to say goodbye to my son.

As we made a beeline for our cars, the group of people outside started closing in on us. This was when I realised just how bad the campaign of hate towards me was. These people began shouting insults right at me; words like 'slag!' and 'murderer!' A man who I recognised as the cousin of Darren's father leant forward and shouted: 'Where have you been the last eight weeks?'

'In the fucking hospital!' I shouted angrily.

I just looked at them all in disgust. I was at my son's funeral in a wheelchair! How dare they imply all this was my fault?

I looked around expecting to see the police that had been promised to us and there were none. All I could see was a couple of community support officers who had no power of arrest. No wonder these people were behaving this way – they had come to cause trouble and there was absolutely nothing to stop them.

There were a couple of steps down to the pavement so Jayne handed me my crutches and helped me up out of my chair so I could get down them. As I was doing this, the stepson of Darren's friend Richard got right in my face shouting 'slag!' at the top of his voice. I glared at him and he spat on me. Can you believe it? A teenage boy kills himself and people turn up to the funeral to spit on the grieving mother. It still disgusts me to this day. The worst criminals on earth would have had more respect than that.

The heckling and taunting rang in our ears until we were in the safety of the funeral cars with the doors locked. The drivers got us out of there as quickly as they could and set off to the crematorium. I telephoned a police officer who was familiar with my case and told him that some real officers had better get there as soon as possible. My terrified mother – who said I was like wounded prey being attacked by a pack of hyenas – was in the car behind me making a 999 call and I know there were other mourners who did the same.

As we travelled down the bypass we realised we were being overtaken. The gang of troublemakers from the funeral were now in cars, racing to beat us to the crematorium. I tried to keep my head: I knew that the police headquarters was right opposite the crem, and after the phone calls that had just been made surely they would be there to make arrests.

Twenty minutes after leaving the church we arrived. The mob had already taken their positions blocking the space where the hearse and funeral cars would usually park. Mum rang me from the car behind.

'Don't get out, Rachel,' she said. 'Wait for the police.'

I knew she was right. I waited, scanning the faces of every person stood outside. Most of these people I had never seen before in my life. I was told in confidence some weeks later that they had been paid to turn up and cause trouble. I can't say for sure that this was true, but it certainly made a lot of sense.

We spotted the vicar and called him over to our car.

'Can we shut this circus down now?' I asked him. This is what Jack's funeral had become – a disgusting circus.

'I'll try,' he said. He looked so upset.

The members of Darren's family who had been at the church were now at the crematorium and joining the group of troublemakers. I watched as the vicar went over to speak to them. They were holding white carnations and chanting:

'Shame on you! Shame on you!' The vicar asked them to quieten down and have some respect for the occasion. I watched in horror as a member of Darren's family stepped forward and shouted in his face, 'You fucking prick!' I could not believe what I was seeing. Where were the police? Where was the security and support we were promised? We waited and waited but they never came. Not one police officer could come to our aid and we were a four-minute drive away from their headquarters.

The vicar suggested rescheduling for the afternoon but when he looked there were no free slots. With the baying crowd showing no signs of relenting and still no sign of the police, it got to the point where we had no choice but to leave. We moved on to the wake at Gwent Rugby Club, leaving Jack there in the hearse. I was burning up with anger, but with Josh and his friends in the car I had to hold it together. I tried to tell myself that it didn't matter, that it was just an empty shell in that coffin, but my God it still hurt. The whole thing was like a terrible nightmare. When was I going to wake up?

The church had been packed at the start of the day but by late afternoon the numbers had dropped considerably. A lot of people had been too frightened to come to the crematorium and even more dropped off after that. Even Colin gave up and went home: he was just too upset.

It was at the wake that we saw our first police officers. One came to police the mourners and a second one patrolled the area outside. We were glad to see them, of course, but it was too little too late. The day was supposed to be about showing love for Jack, and it was torn to shreds by people who wanted to show hate towards me; people who knew nothing about me; people who should be ashamed of themselves. I know for a fact that Darren would have been absolutely disgusted at the way me and my family were treated that day. If he could have come back from the dead for ten minutes, he would have killed the lot of them.

Chapter Twenty-Three

I hoped Jack's funeral would bring me and my family some comfort but all it did was heap pain upon pain. The vicar contacted me to say he had gone ahead with the service at the crematorium. There were a handful of people there to see it — mostly Darren's family. The vicar said he kept it short because he was afraid he was going to have a riot on his hands. I tried to draw strength from the closeness Jack and I shared, but how does a mother reckon with not being there for her son's final moments?

The vicar said I could collect Jack's ashes when I was ready. I decided there and then I was going to keep them for myself. I knew that the spot in the woods where half of Darren's ashes had been scattered was now laden with cards and flowers. I wasn't going to scatter Jack somewhere for people who hated me and my family to use as a shrine.

At a time when I should have been grieving, I was submitting written complaints to the police about the lack of police presence at the funeral. A number of other mourners did the same, including my mother who was absolutely distraught by what happened. She was demanding to know why we didn't get the police support we were promised. I also had to get solicitors involved because Darren's sister Rachael was refusing to return the Land Rover. I started to wonder if all this would ever end.

There were days everything got too much, but I would always pick myself up, dust myself off and put my armour back on. I had to be hard Rachel, just like I was when I was with Darren. I was very driven to push myself forward and just get on with things. I wanted to prove to the world I was coping.

Even so, it was a pretty bold move to sign up to Match.com a few weeks after Jack's funeral. Maybe I saw it as a way of taking back some control of my life. Nothing was going to stop me thinking about Jack, but the pain of losing him had been all-encompassing. I needed a distraction – something positive to focus on. I told myself I could either be pitiful or powerful, and of course I chose powerful.

Everyone I told thought I was mad and that it was far too soon. My girlfriends assured me that I was fabulous and could have anyone I wanted when I was fit, well and in a better place. I knew they were talking sense, but I was marooned in the house by myself most days. I wasn't moping around feeling sorry for myself, but Josh had friends and a life, and Jayne had finally listened to me and gone home to her husband and teenage daughters. Plus, how else was I going to meet someone? Imagining what Darren was really up to all those years he worked the door, remembering the infection he caught and probably passed on to me, well, the thought of going on the pull in pubs and nightclubs made me want to be sick. I thought at the very least I might meet some men who could become friends. A boyfriend would just be a bonus. Of course, there was always the fear I might end up with another Darren – I thought he was The One once remember. But I knew that I was stronger and wiser now. I had to hold on to that and believe that not all men were like him. I had Josh to think about too. He looked up to me and maybe, if I was holding it together and moving forward, he could draw some strength from that.

On my dating profile I stated that I was widowed and had been through a few life-changing experiences over the last few weeks. Although that was probably putting it rather mildly, I wanted to be truthful without scaring anybody off. I had a fair amount of what some people might call baggage and I wanted to be upfront from the start. I started receiving messages from other singles almost immediately. All the men who contacted me seemed very pleasant. Oddly, not one of them questioned what I had written in my profile or tried to find out more. God knows why – maybe they were all too polite.

A few emails were exchanged and I agreed to dates with my two favourites. The first was a fireman, but sadly he didn't set anything alight. The second was with a man who looked absolutely nothing like his profile picture and came across as a bit needy. The last thing I wanted was another needy man. I told him it was nice to meet him but that I didn't see it going any further. I knew how precious time was and I wasn't about to start wasting mine on something that wasn't right for me.

I arrived home after that second date to quite a lengthy email in my inbox. It was from a single man called Mike, a project manager in his early forties. He said he was currently going through a divorce and that he had four children – three with his first wife and one with his second. He said he was sorry to hear I was a widow. I studied his profile picture – he was good-looking with dark hair and nice eyes. So far so good! I wrote a brief email back, thanking him for getting in touch and suggesting that he google me. If he was to read all the coverage of the shooting I was putting all my cards on the table straight away and could leave it up to him whether he wanted things to go any further. He replied straight away saying: 'I won't be googling you. God put eyes in the front of our heads to look forward, not back. I want to get to know you, not read about you. What are you doing this evening? I live twenty minutes from you. If you would like to go out for a meal, give me a call and I will pick you up.'

I got straight on the phone to Nat, my dating-site wing-woman. I was running every man I liked past her and making sure she knew exactly where I was if I met anyone – all on the agreement that she didn't tell our mother! I sent Nat the login details for my Match account so she could have a nosey at Mike's profile.

'What do you think?' I asked her.

'I think you should call him,' she said. 'Say yes to the date!'

So that's what I did. I picked up the phone without a shred of apprehension or nerves and dialled Mike's number.

'Hello?' He sounded so posh with his English accent.

'Hiya, it's me, Rachel.'

We chatted briefly and arranged for Mike to pick me up at seven o'clock. He said he knew a lovely Thai restaurant in Chipping Sodbury, near where he lived in Bristol. I explained that I was currently on crutches as I was recovering from a leg injury. I didn't want him to be shocked when he saw me.

With the arrangements made, I got myself upstairs to get ready. I had less time than I would have liked as I was still struggling to do things like getting washed and dressed. Everything took a lot longer than it would normally. But as I picked out an outfit and put on my make-up, I realised I had butterflies. This feeling was a huge first for me. I can't explain why this date felt so different to the other two, but something in my gut told me it was.

Mike's white Audi pulled up outside my house, bang on time. I closed the door behind me and, using the bend in my good leg, slowly made my way up the steps to the road. It was dark, but as Mike had parked underneath the street light I could see him clearly as he got out of his car to greet me. *Yes!* I thought. He was just as good-looking as his profile picture.

'Hello,' he said in his very English accent.

'Hiya!' I said in my very Welsh accent.

He came round and opened the passenger-side door for me. After making sure I was in the car safely, he took my crutches and placed them on the back seat. As he climbed back into the driver's seat I got a whiff of his aftershave. He smelled gorgeous! My tummy did a little flip. He looked good, smelt good and was behaving like a complete gentleman. This Mike with the English accent was ticking all the boxes so far.

Whenever you meet someone new there is always the fear that you won't have anything in common or that there might be awkward silences. Thankfully, it didn't take me long to realise there would be no such awkwardness between me and Mike. It was a 45-minute drive to the restaurant and – fair enough, I did most of the talking – but we didn't struggle for conversation once. For months now every single thought and conversation had revolved around Darren, the shooting, my leg, the police and then poor Jack. It felt lovely to be around someone completely unattached to all that. For a moment, I could almost forget that I was going through the worst thing that could happen to a mother. I wanted to tell Mike about Jack – it didn't feel right not addressing this when the loss was still so raw in my heart, but I held back. I would pick my moment and tell Mike at dinner.

The restaurant he chose was lovely and quiet enough for us to continue getting to know each other. He told me all about his two marriages and his lovely children. He had two daughters – Olivia and Amelia. His youngest son was called Henry and the eldest, coincidentally, was another Josh! Mike confessed that when we first spoke over the phone he was shocked by the strength of my accent. He said I spoke so fast he struggled to understand a word I was saying!

Naturally, the conversation turned to me and my situation; why was I single? Why was I on crutches? I did my best to keep it honest but brief. I told Mike I'd been in a relationship with a man who struggled with depression and anxiety and that the relationship had been violent for a very long time. I told him that I had finally built up the strength to leave, only for Darren to try to kill me. I also told him that our son, Jack, had taken his own life as a result of what happened.

I was very matter of fact and certainly didn't show much emotion. After 18 years with Darren I had no problem keeping my guard up. I was intensely private about my grief and I'd only just met this man after all. But it was so nice to talk – about Jack in particular – to someone who wasn't my family, someone who wasn't as hurt as I was about the events of the past few months. I was still going through every mother's worst nightmare, but coming to dinner with Mike had brought me some much needed respite from the bubble of grief I'd been lost inside.

'I'm so sorry you've had to go through all this,' Mike said sympathetically.

'It is what it is,' I said, my armour firmly on. 'I'm here, I'm getting on with things. I don't want pity. I just want to try to live my life.'

It was a relief to get my story out in the open. The whole thing was too big a skeleton to keep in the closet. I was looking out for signs I might have scared Mike off, but judging by his body language he didn't seem like he was ready to make a run for it. He was a good listener who seemed genuine and caring.

'I don't think I'll be needing these then,' I said, pulling out my police locator and the six-inch knife I'd been carrying in my bag. Mike's eyes nearly popped out of his head. This must have been quite shocking for someone who had never encountered any type of violence. But to me it was perfectly reasonable. I was on crutches and couldn't move very fast. How else was I going to defend myself?

It was Guy Fawkes Night and as Mike drove me home there were dozens of fireworks popping away on the skyline. We pulled into Brynglas Drive and I wondered if I should invite him in for coffee. He was facing a fairly long drive home, but would it seem too forward? And how would Josh feel about me going on a date and bringing the guy back?

As we parked outside my house, Josh pulled up behind us in a friend's car. There was no avoiding the situation now. I gestured to Josh and he came over to Mike's car.

'Josh, this is Mike,' I said. 'He's coming in for coffee, if that's OK, love?'

Josh being Josh just shrugged. 'Whatever, Mum,' he smiled.

Mike came inside and I made us a cup of coffee. Then we had another and another. We talked on the sofa until Saturday night turned into Sunday morning. Mike eventually said he should be getting off. He had arranged to go to church later that morning with his three eldest children, something he had recently started doing again after a ten-year break.

We said our goodbyes and agreed we would both like to keep in touch. True to his word, Mike sent me a text straight after he had been to a Sunday service. His church-going didn't put me off at all, even though it wasn't something I had ever been into myself. The closest I'd come to religion was a few sessions of Sunday school and, to be honest, I only went for the free squash and biscuits.

Mike said he wanted to see me again.

'Are you free Monday night?' he asked. 'I was thinking you could come here and I'll cook us a meal.'

I nearly fell off my chair: *a man offering to cook for me?* Darren barely cooked me a single meal in the whole 18 years we were together. I could count on one hand the amount of times he made me a cup of coffee and he always put sugar in it, even though I didn't take any.

I agreed to Mike's offer of a second date and that Monday his Audi appeared outside my house, again at seven o'clock on the dot. We drove to his home in Bristol, a house that he owned but had been renting out for years. He had recently moved back in following the breakdown of his second marriage. The interior was cosy and welcoming. Mike sat me down in a recliner chair so I could put my bad leg up. He poured me a glass of wine and placed it on a little side table so my drink would be within easy reach. It was too soon to tell if he was going out of his way to make a good impression or if he was always this thoughtful, but I was in my element. He put something I liked on the TV and disappeared into the kitchen to prepare the meal. While he cooked, we were able to chat through the two adjoining rooms. I felt so comfortable here, with him. *I could get used to this!* I thought.

The night went from strength to strength when he presented me with a beautiful meal of monkfish wrapped in Parma ham, served with stuffed peppers. I was blown away and the food tasted as good as it looked. We talked and talked as if we had known each other for years. I couldn't believe I had found such a lovely man. He was my third date through Match and it was all a wonderful case of third time lucky.

After that night we were constantly in touch with messages flying back and forth. Mike asked if I would like to go with him to meet his old friend, Angela – a Welsh lady who had been Mike's youth church leader when he was young. After not seeing him for some 15 years, she tracked down his number and had contacted him on his birthday a few weeks before we met. Angela said she had a message for Mike – a message from God that she couldn't shake off. In a text she told him: 'God loves you. You are precious to him and he wants you back. But your time is short.' Mike understandably wanted to find out more. Angela only lived around 45 minutes from me so I agreed I would happily go with him.

Two days before our meeting with Angela, I was at home resting my leg. It was aching, but the district nurse was no longer having to come and change my dressing every day. My scar was healing well and I had managed to steer clear of any infections. My main problem was getting enough rest. I was still trying to do everything at 100 miles an hour, still trying to do things my body wasn't quite ready for.

That evening I was lying on the sofa reflecting on the last few months. Grief is like a rollercoaster – when you have one good day it tricks you that you're getting better, only to hit you with several bad. In my low moments, the shooting and Jack's suicide would play out like a horror film in my mind. Then the reality would hit me all over again: Jack was gone and he was never coming back. I never cried in public. I bottled up my tears until I was ready to cry alone. To the outside world I was hard Rachel, yet when I was with Mike I could feel my armour starting to melt away. He didn't judge and he talked sense. He was a breath of fresh air in a world that seemed to be full of anger and bitterness. I was worn out with it all. I didn't want to be hard Rachel any more.

There was a knock at the door. I wasn't expecting Mike but because of the time something told me it was him. I suddenly had this overwhelming feeling that he was here to break up with me. Why else would he turn up unannounced?

Josh came down from his room to answer the door and, sure enough, Mike was standing there. He came through to the living room as Josh disappeared back upstairs.

'I knew it was you,' I said. 'And I know why you're here.'

He looked upset. He sat down on the sofa, put his arm around me and looked into my eyes.

'I can't do this,' he said.

'Do you want a cup of tea before you go?' I said, cutting him off and getting up. My armour was back on.

I made us a drink, thinking, *Well, if you're here to dump me just bloody well get on with it!* When I sat back down, Mike put his arm around me again. He started to explain that having received the text from Angela and recently gone back to church that he had had a real encounter with God.

'This might sound crazy,' he said, 'but I need to put God first in my life. I've never done this before but I have to put God first and let you go. I need to do this wholeheartedly without any distractions.'

I had been expecting him to say 'you're too messed up', or 'I can't handle the baggage'. But no, it was a God thing. I stared at him, puzzled. *Did he really just say he was choosing God over me?*

Sensing my confusion, Mike reached for my laptop.

'Can I show you something?'

He opened the website for his church in Bristol and found a link to a podcast.

'Will you listen to this with me?' he asked.

It was the sermon he'd listened to on his very first visit back to a church in over ten years – a visit that had taken place around the same time as Jack's funeral. I agreed to let him play it to me. I am very open-minded and would never dismiss something without experiencing it myself. We sat side by side, listening to a man talking. I was only taking snippets of it in, but I started to feel a bit strange.

Mike paused the podcast saying he wanted me to listen to the last bit by myself. He then found another clip by a Welshman called Rob Parsons who runs a charity near my home. Again, I agreed to listen. This one was about peace, and it really struck a chord with me. I felt what I can only describe as a warm glow around me, and before I knew what was happening tears were streaming down my cheeks. I looked at Mike and he was crying too. When it was over he wrapped his arms around me and hugged me for several minutes, like he didn't want to let go. When he left, I listened to the end of the first clip like he'd asked: it was about the Sinner's Prayer. Apart from the occasional wedding, I've always associated church with death and funerals. It stirred up a lot of emotion about Jack and I sat there sobbing my heart out.

Later that night I ran myself a bath thinking a good soak would help me relax. While the water was running, I found myself feeling curious about all this church business. I put the laptop back on and started searching through other sermons, clicking on any that looked like they might appeal to me. After listening to a few snippets, I climbed into the bath and closed my eyes. I can't remember why or what I said, but as I lay there in the bubbles, I started to pray. I felt a rush of warmth come over me. I know what you're thinking – I was in a hot bath! But this was a different kind of warmth – not on the outside of my body but on the inside. My emotions overwhelmed me again and I just cried and cried and cried. This was the first time I had truly let go. I didn't know what it was, but I knew something was happening.

Chapter Twenty-Four

Later that night, after my bath and my strange, emotional experience, Mike rang to check I was OK.

'Did you listen to the end of the sermon like I said?' he asked.

I told him I had and that I had been overcome by a kind of internal warmth as I lay in the bath afterwards. I felt comforted by his call and slept well that night, but the next morning I woke up feeling angry. I felt that Mike had led me on and given me false hope of something more serious between us. The more I thought about how lovely and caring he had been, the more pissed off I was. I sent Mike a text and told him I was going to delete his mobile number and email. I didn't know them by heart so it would mean I wouldn't be able to contact him unless he wanted to contact me first. I was quite abrupt and maybe even a bit nasty, but I ended the message with: 'You know where I am if you change your mind,' just in case he ever did.

That evening the phone kept ringing. I ignored it a few times because I didn't recognise the number and I'd had so many nuisance calls. But the caller was persistent, eventually deciding to leave a message.

'I know you're upset,' said Mike's voice, 'but I'd still like to take you to Angela's.'

I thought about it for all of two minutes then rang him back.

'Yes,' I said sternly, 'you can pick me up tomorrow as planned.'

So, on Friday, 11 November, Mike came to collect me and we made our way down to Angela's. On the way, he explained that this would be his second trip to see her since she got in touch on his birthday. After she contacted Mike out of the blue, he agreed to attend her church – partly under duress and partly out of respect for Angela.

'I really wasn't expecting it,' Mike said, 'but something about the service really stirred me.'

I laughed to myself. *What's he on about?* I thought. *Who stirred him? And with what?*

Mike carried on, explaining a bit more about his history with the church. Both of his parents were Christians and his dad used to be an elder at their church. Despite growing up with the Christian faith, Mike had found himself turning his back on the church for the last ten years or so. He had left his first wife and had a string of relationships that led nowhere. He said he was no longer interested in attending church and being around 'God people', and yet, somehow, he never lost his belief in God.

'What made you turn away from the church?' I wondered aloud.

He said some of his fellow church members had written awful letters to him when he left his first wife and children.

'They were so nasty, I just wanted to wash my hands of it all after that,' he said.

We arrived at Angela's and met Rob, her second husband. She had been widowed many years ago and then remarried. We got talking and I felt so comfortable that I opened up about everything that had happened to me that year. Angela got very emotional listening to my story. She said she had seen a lot of it on the news, but meeting me in the flesh and hearing it first-hand had been an altogether different experience.

'Why don't you tell Angela what happened, the night you were in the bath,' Mike said.

I explained about the feeling, about the warmth and the tears. Angela just smiled knowingly as she listened. 'Oh, that's the Holy Spirit,' she said matter-of-factly.

Mike then talked about the day he came to break up with me, saying he had felt the Holy Spirit in my home. When he hugged me goodbye he had been quietly praying to God under his breath that I would find happiness and have a blessed future, and suddenly had a picture in his head of us together. He said the Bible story of Abraham and Isaac had come to him. God tested Abraham's love by asking him to sacrifice Isaac – his only son. Mike was trying to say that I was his Isaac, as he was going to give me up and put God first. I would eventually understand what he meant, but how I kept a straight face in front of everyone that night, God himself only knows! The upshot of it all was that Mike felt God wanted us to be together. We weren't breaking up after all.

That weekend Mike asked me to go to church with him and I said yes. I was beginning to understand his relationship with his faith and after the events of the last few days I was more than a little curious. I was still on crutches and wearing my leg brace when Mike drove us to Woodlands Church, Bristol, and parked near the entrance. There were all sorts of people flocking inside – not just pensioners, but children and adults from all walks of life. I thought back to the free squash and biscuits at Sunday school and wondered if we'd get free tea and coffee. To my delight, there was tea, coffee *and* squash, as well as piles of delicious pastries. *Well,* I thought, eyeing them up, *it was worth coming just for one of those!*

A lot of my preconceptions about church were broken that day. It was a beautiful building with heaters to keep out the chill. The pastor was dressed in jeans and a gilet and had an earring in one ear. The hymns were nothing like I was used to – they were more like pop songs, accompanied by a band with keyboards, guitars and drums. It was actually a very pleasant and surprisingly uplifting morning.

With our fledgling relationship now back on track, I escaped to Mike's place and went to church with him most weekends. With so much still going on between Darren's family and the police, it was wonderful to have Mike and somewhere to get away from it all. I would always make sure Josh was OK and that he was with his girlfriend, Emma. They had been separated when the shooting happened but got back together after Jack died. I always loved Emma and was pleased Josh had another good-hearted person to lean on.

It was my fortieth birthday coming up and, while I knew I could never fully celebrate without Jack there, I decided that I wanted to turn it into something positive, something in his name that would give back to the community. Nat and I got our heads together and decided to hold a charity night. We wrote letters and made phone calls to every organisation we could think of to call in items for an auction. Our top prizes were a Manchester United shirt signed by striker Javier Hernandez, a pair of signed gloves from local boxing hero Joe Calzaghe, and signed rugby balls from our beloved local teams. We contacted the Hilton Hotel, who let us book their ballroom at a discounted rate and even let us throw in an overnight stay as a raffle prize! We were blown away by people's generosity and, as word spread, tickets to the event sold like hot cakes.

Before the end of November, I had the brace taken off my leg and finished my course of weekly physio. That December, four months after the shooting, I walked into a hospital appointment without using my crutches. My surgeon could not believe what he was seeing.

'I told you I wouldn't be like this for long!' I said.

After that I got rid of everything in my house that made me feel like a victim – the Zimmer frame, the commode and the seats over the toilets. I knew that because of my titanium knee there were things I would never be able to do. I will always have limited bend in my left leg now, which means I struggle to walk down steps properly and I will never be able to run or ride a bike. I can't ever go back to full-time hairdressing because I can't stand for long periods of time. I won't be able to drive a manual car either, but I got round that by ordering myself a nice little automatic. It was important to me to get back on the road and retain some independence.

At the end of January 2012, I received a letter from Detective Superintendent Mark Warrender of the Professional Standards Department at Cwmbran Police Headquarters. A review had been carried out in the wake of formal complaints from me and my family about what we felt was the shambolic policing of Jack's funeral. In it, the police acknowledged that there were 'significant tensions' between Jack's family and that it was clear the funeral was going to be 'an emotional and highly charged focal point.' Prior to the day, they developed a policing plan to provide a measured response 'empathetic to the emotional tensions'. Intervention was only to occur in extreme situations and minor matters would be investigated afterwards. In the review of the case, Chief Superintendent Julian Knight wrote that he had 'reflected' on whether anything could have been done differently and his conclusion was, no!

> *I believe that both the strategy, the policing style adopted and the execution of the operational order achieved that very difficult balance identified as necessary in the plan. We did create the appropriate space for the natural outpouring of grief from a very difficult family situation and still prevented serious public disorder or serious violence to any mourners present.*

The official summary was: no one got hurt so the police did their job. The review also stated that what *I* was expecting that day and what they were actually planning on delivering were two very different things. For that, I received an apology.

> *It is absolutely clear to me that your expectations of the police role during the course of the funeral were not met and for this I would offer my sincerest apologies on behalf of Gwent Police. Falling short of your expectations was either through miscommunication, misunderstanding or both. In any event the precise strategy for policing the funeral should have been*

explained to you and your understanding of what was to happen from the police perspective checked and clarified.

I am confident that some important learning will come out of this experience for the police, but regret that you were unable to properly mourn your son's tragic loss.

On 12 February 2012, the night of the charity function, I arrived at the venue around an hour before the party was scheduled to start. When Nat told me that she had spotted Darren's Land Rover parked on the roundabout outside, my heart sank. After the months of online abuse, petty crime and nuisance phone calls, I couldn't rule out more of the kind of trouble we'd encountered at Jack's funeral. I called the police straight away. As far as I knew, Darren's sister Rachael still had possession of the vehicle. I could only assume it was her or Wayne, or at the very least someone who knew them. Thankfully, the police came and swiftly moved the Land Rover on. After that they took no more chances, patrolling outside the venue until the event had finished.

It was an amazing night. The music was provided by one of my favourite bands – Big Mac's Wholly Soul Band – who did the gig for half price. We raised £2,200 in all, donating £1,000 to Morriston Hospital as a thank you for my treatment, £700 to the local Bobby Van scheme who kitted my bedroom out with security measures, and £500 in Jack's name to Winston's Wish – a charity for bereaved children.

I came away from the event feeling rejuvenated with an even stronger sense of purpose. Maybe something good would come out of all this. Maybe my life could begin at 40 after all.

Chapter Twenty-Five

With the first anniversary of Jack's death fast approaching, I asked Mike if we could think about going away somewhere. I was determined to mark the day as a celebration of his life and not let it be a sad day. I discussed the idea with Josh, who said he would very much like to join us. He also wanted to bring along his girlfriend Emma. The four of us planned a week's holiday to Cyprus so we would be away for Jack's anniversary. Coincidentally, the day Jack took his life – 26 September – was also the birthday of Mike's son Josh, who was turning 18 that year. Mike explained the situation to him and he insisted he was fine to see his dad another time.

We arrived in Paphos with a few days to settle in and enjoy the sun. On the morning of the anniversary, I decided that I would like to head down to the local harbour and have a look around. The four of us jumped in a taxi and asked the driver to take us somewhere we could grab breakfast. He dropped us at a gorgeous little café right down the front. We had breakfast staring out at the boats moored in the harbour and the lovely views out to sea. We talked non-stop about our little Jack Sparrow, how he loved the water and how he used to tell me he was going to sail around the world one day. Afterwards, we had a stroll around the harbour. I had talked about getting myself a pair of diamond earrings so, when we stumbled upon a little jewellery shop, Mike stopped to look in the window. He called me over to show me a ring he had spotted, but I dismissed him. I wanted earrings not a ring.

A lady came out of the shop to ask if Mike needed any help.

'Could I have a look at this ring?' he asked, disappearing inside.

I was trying not to go in as I didn't want Mike spending money on me, but I also didn't want to appear rude. When I stepped inside the shop all the shop assistants were smiling at me. Mike was sat down looking at a ring and as I got closer I realised what it was: a diamond engagement ring with a stunning marquise diamond.

'Try it on!' Mike said.

'How much is it?' I asked, panicking about the price.

'Never mind that,' he laughed. 'Just try it on.'

Heart thumping, I slipped it onto my ring finger. It fit perfectly. As I stood there, admiring my hand with this incredible diamond catching the light, Mike explained the poignancy of the day to everyone in the shop. Within five minutes the staff were in tears. I looked at Mike and then Emma to find they were both crying too. Josh and I ended up trying to comfort them all! This was all very emotional and unexpected, but it also felt very right. I also knew that, had Jack been here, he would have approved of Mike and me being together.

Once everyone had pulled themselves together, Mike paid for the engagement ring. We also bought our wedding bands from there, to use at a later date. Mike wasn't messing about! I left that shop happier than I had been in a very long time. The whole day had a sense of one chapter of my life leading into the next.

That night we sipped cocktails on the beach and watched the sun go down. We toasted Jack's life and Mike's son's birthday, then agreed to keep the engagement news between us. With Mike still waiting for his divorce to be finalised, we had to wait a few months before making it official. Even though my diamond had to be put away in a drawer for now, I came home from Paphos a very happy woman. I could feel Jack in my heart and a bright future ahead of me.

Chapter Twenty-Six

Since the shooting and Jack's suicide, there had been several major inquiries to address complaints and identify potential failings, and at the end of November 2012 a series of reports were made public. In one of them, the Independent Police Complaints Commission publicly criticised Gwent Police for the way they handled my case and upheld four complaints against them. These included my complaints that the police took too long to arrest Darren after I made my statement on 25 July about him strangling me some two weeks earlier, and that they did not investigate claims Darren had breached his bail, despite being told he was in a gym a mile away from me and had poured bleach on my clothes.

The report found that, once I had gone to the police on 25 July, key risk information was not available to the people managing me and Darren. This meant that the Serious Violent Crimes Unit and the Domestic Abuse Unit were not aware of Darren's bail breaches. The report stated: 'It is possible that Darren Williams would have been remanded in custody if the breaches were pursued and evidenced.'

Officers on the ground were not made aware that I was high risk or that Darren was a high-risk offender, because 'information was not always coordinated and considered as a whole'. In another cock-up, after I gave my statement on 25 July, an officer was advised to post a handover file via Gwent Police's internal mail and it did not reach the Serious Violent Crimes Unit until 1 August. This explains why the police were so slow to arrest Darren. It also completely contradicts the fact that the Serious Violent Crimes team only deal with high-risk cases. Had they moved more quickly, they could have intervened in Darren's plans for a rampage at the salon. To add insult to injury, the calls me and my mum made to the police were not even logged properly. There were nearly forty different police officers involved in our case over a six-week period and none of them knew what the others were doing. Because of limited resources, a lack of consistency and huge pitfalls in communication and operational systems, the situation was free to escalate as it did. The report said: 'No single officer or other professional had an overview of the escalating situation. Each incident was dealt with according to the presenting situation. Events also moved on so quickly that one had not been fully investigated before the next occurred.'

Jack's death prompted a Serious Case Review, analysing how Gwent Police, Aneurin Bevan Health Board and Newport City Council had dealt with events. The author of the review, Ruby Parry, admitted there had been shortcomings in how the case was handled. Just like the police, these authorities had also failed to share relevant and important information with each other. Again, everyone was doing their bit but no one knew the full picture.

I was also the subject of a Domestic Homicide Review. Mine was the first of its kind in Newport – although it's not an accolade anyone wants and, sadly, it wasn't the last. Shockingly, my case highlighted the fact that Gwent Police and myself – a high-risk victim of domestic violence – were not made aware of the court hearing to vary Darren's bail restrictions. This meant magistrates were clueless to the fact that he had already breached his original terms. Had we been given the opportunity to provide them with an update, Darren would almost certainly have been remanded in custody instead of being free to try to kill me. The Crown Prosecution Service said that they would usually notify the Witness Care Team, and yet there was no record of it happening in this case, despite the defendant being a man with a history of violence, suicide and mental-health problems. To this day, I still don't understand why Darren changed his bail restrictions or why he got his wish.

To focus on the positives: recommendations for change were made across the board with a view to improving communication for future cases and hopefully to stop any other young person falling through the cracks the way Jack did. I suppose, ultimately, these reports confirmed what I already knew: that Darren and Jack and I were let down by the system. As painful as it was, I had found myself in the unusual position of having to accept that sometimes mistakes have to happen before real change can be made.

The TV show *This Morning* had tried to approach me several times since the shooting. They had been in touch with Jane from *Wales News* on the back of her involvement with me, hoping I would agree to an interview. With the case back in the spotlight because of the recent reports, I decided that, if they still wanted me, it would be a good time to make my TV debut.

Jane helped make the necessary arrangements and I set off on the train to London with the other Jayne in my life for support. When we arrived at the ITV studios we couldn't believe we were there. Like a couple of schoolgirls we took photographs then sat in the green room feeling like VIPs. Unfortunately, it didn't go completely smoothly. News that I was going to appear on the show had reached Darren's family and, when a production assistant came in and said they'd had an email from Spain, I knew immediately it was from Darren's mother. She wanted to make sure that I was not going to speak about Darren's affair or his secret son. I didn't like being told what to do, but I had no intention of bringing up Isobele or her son Josh on TV anyway.

The interview was a success. Presenters Holly Willoughby and Phillip Schofield were lovely and, even though it was nerve-racking doing my first live TV, I realised there's nothing to be nervous about when you're telling your own story because you know it inside out!

Mike and I had been a couple for over a year now. He was a huge comfort and support as I slowly came to terms with the fateful events of 2011 and the fall-out that came with it. We did an Alpha Course together and made many new friends through the church. If you had told me years ago that I would be going to church and enjoying spending time with God people, I would have laughed in your face. And yet here I was. I wouldn't really say that I found God – it felt more like God had found me. I didn't have to be hard Rachel any more. I now had love and strength within me that was deeper than that.

In January 2013, Mike read an email that had been sat in his inbox unopened for almost a week. His divorce had been finalised. As we sat snuggled up on the sofa watching a film, he turned to me and said, 'How do you feel about getting the ring out?'

'Ooh yeah!' I squealed, and we went upstairs to get it.

He playfully asked me to marry him and I pretended to hesitate for a moment. We were so happy and secure that we knew very early on that marriage was on the cards. Mike assured me that after two failed marriages he would not be putting himself through it all again unless he was absolutely sure it was going to last. My family must have thought I was mad getting into another relationship so quickly – not that I would have listened if anyone tried to stop me! Thankfully, I think they could see from the off that Mike was not another Darren. He literally couldn't be further from it! I was finally in a good place and the road ahead was filled with promise.

Nearly two years on from the shooting, inquests for Darren's and Jack's suicides were still pending. By this time, Rachael and I were back on speaking terms. She had made contact and I was willing to forgive her and Wayne, letting them keep and sell the Land Rover to put towards the funeral bill still hanging over them. She explained that she had been angry about my one-night stand with Gareth and desperate to salvage Darren's name. She had also taken my refusing to let Jack come and collect his belongings as a sign I had disowned him. I understood that emotions had been high and conclusions were jumped to. Her last memory of Darren was him sobbing his heart out in her spare room.

During our text conversations, I let Rachael know that I knew about Darren's affair with Isobele and their secret son Josh. When we were all invited to the same family function and I heard Isobele couldn't get there, I stepped in and offered her a lift. I know it sounds crazy that I would want to meet someone Darren had an affair with, but I felt it was important to get some closure and assure her there were no hard feelings.

Isobele and I spoke over Facebook and she agreed that I could pick her up. When I arrived at her flat, I came face to face with Darren's son Josh.

'Hiya,' he said sheepishly. 'I'm the dirty little secret.'

'Don't you ever say that,' I told him. 'You've done nothing wrong. You've as much right to be on this earth as anybody else.'

Isobele and I talked briefly. I told her that it had been a huge shock finding out about her, but at the end of the day, Darren was the one who cheated. I didn't hold anything against her.

In June 2013, the inquests into Darren's and Jack's suicides finally went ahead. I was called as a witness to both, but after speaking to my doctor we agreed it could be detrimental to my health and I was excused. Instead, I wrote lengthy statements to be read out in court.

Darren's inquest was 11 June, a chance for his family to hear the full story about the shooting and everything that led up to it. None of my family attended, it was all his. Rachael and Wayne went along and kept me updated by text. Because they were now more sympathetic towards my experience, there were members of their family who felt they were being disloyal. Darren's other sister Lisa attended the hearing, telling the court that on the day before the shooting Darren told her, 'I'm going to get Rachel back for what she did to me. I'm going to get my revenge. I don't want to kill her I want to shoot both her legs. I'm going to go bang bang.'

This was a chilling statement and yet another indication of Darren's twisted logic and state of mind. However, I couldn't help but feel that, by saying he only wanted to shoot me in the legs, Lisa was still trying to claw Darren's name out of the mud. He had threatened to kill me time and time again. He had told me over and over that he couldn't live without me. I am still absolutely sure of the fact that his plan was always to kill me then kill himself. Gwent Coroner David Bowen ruled Darren's death was suicide – a result of his own unassisted action.

Jack's inquest took place the following day. I was told there was a heavy police presence, anticipating problems between Darren's family and my own. The *South Wales Argus* was in court posting updates online in real time. At 10.59am, they reported that an argument had broken out among members of Darren's family and the court had been adjourned. At 11.02am, two family members were escorted out by police. At 11.05am the inquest resumed with the coroner reminding everyone to respect Jack's memory. Just before midday came the verdict: Jack Williams killed himself while depressed. The coroner described it as 'tragic' and said it should never have happened.

I do not blame myself for Jack's death. I was in a hospital over an hour away for five weeks trying to deal with things that were out of my control. I did question myself for a while. *Could I have done more? Was this my fault for staying with Darren all those years?*

These doubts were preyed upon by people who did blame me. But I worked hard to push the negative thoughts from my mind. Beating myself up with 'what ifs' is not going to bring Jack back. I did everything I could to love and help Darren. In the end, I stayed with him as a form of self-preservation so I could be around for my kids. As many people have said to me, there's only one person to blame for Jack's death and that's Darren.

Chapter Twenty-Seven

With the inquests and various reports bringing a certain degree of closure, my thoughts turned to how I could help other women. I had a good relationship with the press and a strong public profile – not just in Wales but across the UK. I wanted to use that as a force for good. I wanted to help all the women still trapped and suffering in violent and abusive relationships.

In 2014 I set up my own Facebook page called Don't Look Back. I saw it as a place women could come to ask for help, support and advice, and, my goodness, they came in their droves. I found myself signposting women to public services day and night. Many women got in touch privately to ask me if they were experiencing domestic abuse, and, sadly, I believe almost all of them were. It's awful to think women don't even know when they are being abused, but I was one of those women! Abusers are clever and confusing creatures who aren't necessarily monsters 100 per cent of the time. One young woman described how her partner had bought her a dog – something she accepted as a loving gesture from a man who was serious about her. And yet it became a form of control: he would threaten to hurt the dog if she didn't do what he wanted. Just like me all those years ago, she couldn't really equate the kind man with the controlling man. She believed that if he was nice some of the time then he couldn't be all bad. Sadly, once you believe that, an abuser has you right where they want you.

Putting myself out there on social media meant my Facebook page did attract a number of unwanted comments from people still hell-bent on bringing me down, but I did what I had now programmed myself to do – let it wash over me and report it to the police. I was turning my mess into my message, and I wasn't going to let anyone break my stride. Sadly, through talking to other survivors I have learnt that it is now part and parcel for victims to have to deal with additional torment from their abuser's family and friends, whether that's face to face or on social media. As if these women don't go through enough already.

Keen to build on the success of my Facebook page, in 2015 I contacted Welsh Women's Aid. I didn't really understand what it was they did or how I could help, but they were delighted to hear from me and asked if I would like to speak at their annual Light a Candle service that November. I said yes, absolutely clueless to the magnitude of what I was signing up for.

That May, Mike and I finally tied the knot. The weather was horrendous for a full week beforehand as well as the morning itself. But I didn't have time to waste fretting – our wedding day was also polling day so I had to call into the local school to cast my vote en route to the church. I certainly got a few strange looks as I ran inside wearing my wedding dress, but knowing first-hand how important it is to have people in power that want to stamp out domestic abuse, I was more politically charged than I'd been my whole life. I tweeted a picture of myself at the ballot box which was picked up by the local paper. Hilariously, I ended up headline news again, this time on my wedding day.

By the time I got to the church the sky was blue and the sun was shining. We had over a hundred guests, a full sit-down meal and a live band in the evening. We held a collection for the Ride for Hope event run by our church and raised over £200. I spent the day smiling from ear to ear and feeling like a bride should. Jack was sorely missed, but Josh was so happy to see me happy. I got my dream wedding and my dream man.

A month after the wedding, Welsh Women's Aid appointed me an ambassador for their Children Matter programme, which aims to highlight the effect abuse has on children who grow up around it. Because I'd lost Jack in such terrible circumstances, they felt I would be a strong face for the campaign that other mothers could relate to.

It's only now, doing the work that I do, that I understand just how much children are affected by violence in the home. They might not see everything, but sometimes that's worse because what they don't see they make up in their heads. If I'd known this when my boys were young, maybe I would have tried to leave Darren sooner. There is no escaping the fact that a series of violent events over many years contributed to Jack's mental state when he took his own life.

In November 2015, I prepared myself for my first speech at the WWA Light a Candle event. In my head I was expecting a small church gathering, but it was at Llandaff Cathedral – a ginormous place! I rocked up on the day with Mike, my sisters, a couple of friends and my speech printed out onto A4 paper. When I saw the cathedral in all its glory, the nerves kicked in. I sat at the front, telling myself there wouldn't be many people, only to hear the chanting of the Women's Aid march as they descended on the grounds ready for the service. I looked round to see women pouring through the doors to take their seats. Before long, the cathedral was packed to the rafters and I was starting to wonder what on earth I was doing! To make matters worse, I was one of the first women to speak. Although a lot of people there would have seen my story on TV and in the press, it was the first time I'd spoken publicly and at length about what happened. As I stood there recounting my relationship with Darren and how he nearly killed me, you could have heard a pin drop. When I finished reading my speech and looked up at the crowd, they rose to their feet clapping and cheering. The local assembly minister Leighton Andrews was next to me in tears. It was an amazing feeling and confirmation that by telling my story I was shining a light on abuse and fighting for change.

On the back of my work with Welsh Women's Aid I was
taken on as an ambassador for Llanelli Women's Aid and started
working with a family and friends survivor group for Safe Lives,
a national charity dedicated to ending domestic abuse for good.
In July 2016, Safe Lives invited me to an event saying they were
expecting a very famous special guest. It was there I met the
Duchess of Cornwall – or Camilla, as we like to call her. She
came and listened to me and a number of other women speak
about our experiences of domestic violence and, to my surprise,
the Duchess was so moved she shed a few tears.

After that, a couple of us got an invite to Clarence House in
London for a function the Duchess was laying on for domestic
abuse services. While we were there, Camilla's secretary
approached me.

'Have you spoken to the Duchess yet?' she asked. 'Let me get
her for you.'

She brought Camilla over and she said, 'Hello, Rachel, how
are you?'

I don't know if she was just well briefed but it felt wonderful
that she remembered my name. Later that day she gave a speech
and as she addressed the crowd she looked at me with a tear in her
eye and repeated something that had inspired her – something I
had said to her the first time we met: 'I'm no longer a victim; I'm
a victor.'

I have since gone on to speak at many more events, including the
2017 Labour Women's Conference. My driving force was always
that if I could help one person I would have succeeded in my
mission, but I know from the feedback I get and the emotional

emails that I have helped hundreds. I have succeeded way beyond my expectations.

While I navigate life in the public eye, I still get the occasional abuse from supporters of Darren's. There are people out there who can't stand to see me move on and do well. But to be honest, they can do whatever they want to me now. The novelty of being free from Darren far outweighs any of the negatives. If I want to wear false eyelashes, I do. If I want to colour my hair, I do. If I want to go up town and get absolutely steaming drunk, I can. I probably won't, but I *could*. I suppose you could say I'm a little bit rebellious. It does mean I can be a bit too harsh on Mike sometimes. I'm giving him my 'how dare you tell me what to do' speech before he's even gone there. But I'm still pinching myself that I can do whatever I want and I never want to take that for granted.

I would be lying if I said I didn't carry any emotional scars from what I've been through. It still feels incredibly strange to be able to talk to other men without having to worry or explain myself. When your mind has been conditioned as mine was for 18 years, it can be quite hard to know what's normal, but I'm finally in a healthy relationship that's built on love, trust and mutual respect.

The physical scars are still there as a daily reminder. I have a large circular scar around my left knee and a line going down my shin. It's not pretty, but I embrace it. In the summer I wear skirts and shorts. The scars are a part of me and a visual reminder of what I survived. If I hadn't pulled my legs up that day, I'm certain the shot from Darren's gun would have killed me. My leg saved my life. And when I think back to when I was told they may have to amputate, I thank God I had my wits about me enough to refuse. I could quite easily have taken their advice and been an amputee and yet here I am still walking around on both legs.

I believe I am living proof that we grow in the dark times; it's the dark times that made me strong. We all go through situations in life we don't deserve or understand. But if we were always in the light, we wouldn't grow into the flowers we are supposed to be.

To all the women reading this who are in a violent relationship, or maybe even in a shelter having escaped one, I want you to know that you are not alone and there is always a way. Keep on reaching out for help until you find it.

In church we sing a song: 'Your tears will dry, your heart will mend, your scars will heal and you will dance again.'

And you too will dance again.

Acknowledgements

I would like to dedicate this book to my sons. First to my darling younger boy Jack, who I know is shining down on me and giving me the strength and courage to fight on to raise public awareness of domestic abuse. Then to my elder son Josh, who has shown tremendous courage, wisdom and resilience throughout these tragic events. Josh, I am so proud of the person you have become. You have not let 19 August 2011, and the aftermath of that day, rob you of your life. We have got through this together.

Then I would like to acknowledge the help, love and support I have had, and continue to have, from family and friends, old and new.

Thank you also to Ellie Piovesana, for helping me to find the right words to tell my story.

Most importantly, I would like to thank God, for without him this would not be possible. He not only saved my life and gave me a second go at it, but he has given me grace to forgive those that need forgiving, and the strength and courage to move forward with my life. He has also given me a wonderful man who has come into my life and stood by me through it all. He has been my shoulder to cry on, scream and shout at and, most importantly, he has shown me what love is.

Thank you all for being part of my journey. I love you all.